T0195803

math education *for* gifted students

math education *for* gifted students

edited by
susan k. johnsen
and
james kendrick

Routledge
Taylor & Francis Group

NEW YORK AND LONDON

First published 2005 by Prufrock Press Inc.

Published 2021 by Routledge
605 Third Avenue, New York, NY 10017
2 Park Square, Milton Park, Abingdon, Oxon OX14 4RN

Routledge is an imprint of the Taylor & Francis Group, an informa business

Library of Congress Cataloging-in-Publication Data

Math education for gifted students /
edited by Susan K. Johnsen and James Kendrick.
        p. cm.— (A Gifted child today reader)
    Includes bibliographical references.
    ISBN 1-59363-166-9
    1. Mathematics—Study and teaching. 2. Gifted children— Identification. 3. Gifted children—Education. I. Johnsen, Susan K. II. Kendrick, James, 1974– III. Series.

    QA11.2.M27 2005
    371.95'37—dc22

                                                            2005018784

ISBN 13: 978-1-59363-166-6 (pbk)

Contents

Overview   ix

Section I
Differentiating Mathematics for Gifted Students

1   Mathematically Gifted Students: 3
    How Can We Meet Their Needs?
    by Jennifer V. Rotigel and Susan Fello

2   Mathematically Gifted in the Heterogeneously   17
    Grouped Mathematics Classroom:
    What Is a Teacher to Do?
    by Catherine Finlayson Reed

3   Catering for Mathematically Gifted Elementary   33
    Students: Learning From Challenging Tasks
    by Carmel M. Diezmann and James J. Watters

Section II
Instructional Strategies
for Teaching Mathematically Gifted Students

4   Tiered Lessons: One Way to Differentiate   49
    Mathematics Instruction
    by Rebecca L. Pierce and Cheryll M. Adams

5   Can Distance Learning Meet the Needs   61
    of Gifted Elementary Math Students?
        by Sylvia St. Cyr

6   Mathematical Acceleration in a Mixed-Ability   83
    Classroom: Applying a Tiered-Objectives Model
        by Todd Kettler and Marc Curliss

7   Breaking Down the Barriers: Adventures   93
    in Teaching Single-Sex Algebra Classes
        by Susan Lee Stutler

8   Math in Architecture: Using Technology   105
    to Connect Math to the Real World
        by Mary Christopher

9   Gifted Students Speak: 119
    Mathematics Problem-Solving Insights
        by Thomas R. Tretter

About the Authors   145

Overview

These articles from *Gifted Child Today* were selected specifically for the teacher who is searching for ways to serve mathematically gifted students in the classroom. This overview provides a brief summary of the authors' major concepts covered in each of the chapters, including (a) characteristics of mathematically gifted students, (b) qualities of teachers who are effective in working with such students, (c) the role of mathematically gifted students in the classroom, (d) attributes of a differentiated curriculum, (e) plans for designing challenging math tasks, and (f) specific strategies for teaching mathematically gifted students.

Mathematically gifted students' talents frequently emerge as early as preschool as they become engaged in challenging tasks. They master basic skills rapidly (Diezmann & Waters), reason quickly (Reed), and frequently answer with unusual speed and accuracy (Rotigel & Fello). They are able to see relationships among concepts and ideas, and they are intuitive about mathematical functions and processes (Rotigel & Fello). They are not satisfied with simply knowing the answer, but rather want to know the how's and why's of mathematical ideas (Rotigel & Fello) and actually prefer tasks that are full of problems and hard questions (Diezmann & Watters; Tretter). Reed classifies these mathematically gifted students into two types: those who are "precocious" and ahead of their peers and those who are "able to solve demanding problems by employing qualitatively different thinking processes" (p. 21).

Teachers who are effective with students who are mathematically gifted are knowledgeable about mathematics. They know how to select challenging tasks, how to facilitate without reducing the complexity of the problem, and how to provide support through scaffolding, modeling, and coaching (Diezmann & Watters).

The student assumes a more active role in the problem-solving process by self-selecting the problem (Reed), deciding on a process to solve the problem, sharing his or her solutions through projects (Rotigel & Fello), and evaluating the solution through metacognitive reflection (Diezmann & Watters). Tretter found that students enjoy courses in which they are able to think creatively, have time to solve more challenging problems, and are able to work collaboratively with other students of similar abilities.

Given gifted students' accelerated and intuitive thought processes regarding mathematics, teachers need to design differentiated curricula and use strategies that increase the complexity and pace of instruction. Kettler and Curliss suggest that gifted students actually retain content with accuracy if taught more quickly and may even mislearn if reviewed more frequently.

Some authors describe differentiated curricula as involving the modification of content, process, and product (Pierce & Adams; Reed). On the other hand, Tretter classifies the modifications according to acceleration, enrichment, sophistication, and novelty. In both cases, the emphasis is on depth over breadth, open-ended problem solving, challenge, and applications in the real world.

In organizing a differentiated curriculum, Rotigel and Fellow suggest that teachers may want to use a more linear structure since pretesting is a key element in many strategies such as compacting, grade skipping, and cluster grouping. Reed supports the need for preassessment to eliminate repetition in the curriculum. Similarly, Kettler and Curliss used preassessment to determine the use of tiered objectives where gifted students learn objectives within a given concept at higher grade levels.

Within the differentiated curriculum, challenging math tasks need to be designed. Diezmann and Waters describe such tasks as having the following characteristics:

1. They are authentic, emulating the practices of mathematicians.
2. They develop mathematical abstract reasoning.
3. They develop metacognitive skills.
4. They enhance motivation.

For learners to develop their mathematical skills and reasoning, the task must then provide for open-ended investigation (Reed) with increasing complexity (Rotigel & Fello) so that the student is challenged, but not frustrated.

The authors in this book provide some specific strategies for both organizing a gifted program and teaching mathematically gifted students in either the general education classroom or in special settings. In terms of organizing a program, Stutler provides evidence that girls who are mathematically gifted may be more successful in single-sex math classes in the middle school than in heterogeneous classes. In her study, the success rate for girls changed from less than 10% in heterogeneous classes (i.e., boys and girls) to 100% in homogeneous, all-girl classes. In terms of strategies, Pierce and Adams explain the use of tiered lessons in which the teacher develops different activities for students who are grouped according to readiness. Cyr describes the use of distance learning in accelerating a precocious student who will be ready for eighth-grade math when he enters junior high school. Christopher shows how to teach math concepts as an integrated whole using math in architecture.

We want to thank the authors for their contributions. We hope you find this book helpful in serving mathematically gifted students in your classroom.

Susan K. Johnsen
James Kendrick
Editors

Differentiating Mathematics for Gifted Students

chapter 1

~

Mathematically Gifted Students
how can we meet their needs?

by **Jennifer V. Rotigel** *and* **Susan Fello**

today, as usual, Mrs. Johnson began her third-grade math class by reading aloud a thinking puzzle: Charlie, the dog, was tied to a 2-meter rope. His favorite ball was lying in the grass at least 10 yards away from him. He managed to grasp the ball easily. How did he manage to do this?

Nathan's hand flew into the air just microseconds after his teacher finished posing the question. While his classmates were pondering the problem, Nathan had already formulated the answer. Surprising even Mrs. Johnson, Nathan immediately found the lateral thinking puzzle required little effort and absolutely no math. While other students were converting meters to yards, moving decimal points, and drawing pictures, Nathan realized that the other end of the rope was not attached to anything; the dog merely had a 2-meter rope tied to his collar, but was not tethered at all.

Whether Nathan had heard the "riddle" before or whether he surmised that mathematics couldn't solve the scenario remains a mystery. Nevertheless, most teachers have had similar experiences with children who are talented in mathematics and strong in logical reasoning. Unfortunately, many programs for gifted children are inadequate and poorly designed (Heid, 1983), leaving classroom teachers struggling to meet the needs of gifted children effectively. What resources are available for these students? What assessment tools are appropriate? Do these children need acceleration or enrichment? How can we meet their needs when there are so many other demands on teachers' time? This chapter will address these and other questions in an attempt to shed some light on the difficult issues of challenging and nurturing children who demonstrate talent in the field of mathematics.

Characteristics of the Gifted Math Student

Whether math problems require computation skills, problem-solving strategies, inferential thinking skills, or deductive reasoning, mathematically talented students are often able to discern answers with unusual speed and accuracy. Mathematically gifted students are able to see relationships among topics, concepts, and ideas without the intervention of formal instruction specifically geared to that particular content (Heid, 1983). Due to their intuitive understanding of mathematical function and processes, they may skip over steps and be unable to explain how they arrived at the correct answer to a problem (Greenes, 1981).

For example, Mariah, an energetic sixth-grade prealgebra student, often seems disinterested during her hour-long math class, as she doodles and appears to be preoccupied. While the teacher demonstrates the steps required for calculating the correct answer to $4b + 11 = 2b + 23$, Mariah leafs through her history folder. After all, she can solve these linear algebraic equations in just one step. Like many gifted students, she barely listens to the teacher's directions, does not write page numbers in her assignment book, and does not make eye contact with the teacher. Mariah views practicing step-by-step processes as a waste of time when solutions can be found by just looking at the problem.

Students who are talented in mathematics often demonstrate an uneven pattern of mathematical understanding and development, since some are much stronger in concept development than they are in computation (Rotigel, 2000; Sheffield, 1994). Gifted math students often to know more about the "hows" and "whys" of mathematical ideas than the computational "how-to" processes (Sheffield). Since these children often prefer to learn all they can about a particular mathematical idea before leaving it for new concepts, a more expansive approach to mathematics based upon student interest may avoid the frustration that occurs when the regular classroom schedule demands that it is time to move on to another topic. A more linear approach to mathematics is often a better match for gifted children instead of the spiral curricula often found in textbook series and followed by classroom teachers. For example, when the topic of decimals is introduced, children with mathematical talent can be allowed to delve much further into the topic, learning practical applications for decimals and the connections between decimals and other mathematical topics.

Many of these students' gifted characteristics emerge during the preschool years. Bailey, a mathematically precocious 5-year-old, understands that numbers have patterns and relationships to real life. While watching a series of movie previews at the local theater, she can skillfully decide which new releases will occur before or after she turns 6 simply by noting their release dates in the upcoming year. Parents of preschoolers may report that their child demonstrates an unusual interest in mathematical concepts and particularly enjoys games involving numbers. At an early age, some gifted students note relationships between products and prices in the grocery store, the passage of time, changes in weather temperatures, and measurements of distances. Parents of these "number sense gurus" are fascinated by their children's precociousness, but are often unaware of the significance or relevance of these early mathematical discoveries.

By the time these emergent mathematical geniuses arrive for their first formal math lessons in kindergarten, they may have already established their own unique theories of number sense, sequences and patterns, problem solving, and computational strategies. Too frequently, the teachers following the curriculum merely touch on many math concepts, failing to recognize and nurture young mathematicians (Pletan, Robinson, Berninger, & Abbott, 1995). Formal instruction in elementary school classrooms often lacks challenge for the gifted learner since courses in regular classrooms tend to have a relatively narrow range of topics, minimal investigation of concepts, repeated drill and practice, and yearly repetition. The basic mathematical concepts that are presented in kindergarten and first grade can be a particular problem for children who have already mastered number recognition, one-to-one correspondence, and counting. Recent studies indicate that few instructional adaptations are made to accommodate these young learners' needs (Archambault, Westberg, Brown, Hallmark, Emmons, & Zhang, 1993). Students gifted in mathematical thinking and problem solving need greater depth and breadth of topics and open-ended opportunities for solving more complex problems (Sheffield, 1994).

Challenges for School Districts

Misunderstandings regarding the nature of giftedness and talent abound, and busy teachers and administrators are sometimes at a loss as to how to nurture and challenge children whose abilities belie their age-based grade-level placement. However, according to the Principles and Standards for School Mathematics (National Council of Teachers of Mathematics, 2000, p. 13), these students must be supported so that they too have an opportunity to reach their mathematical potential. All too often, the regular curriculum is insufficient in depth, breadth, and pace to meet the needs of the gifted child (Wolfle, 1986). In addition, the recent emphasis on state standardized testing programs has increased the use of basic skills instruction and drill in an attempt to assure that all students will be successful on these tests (Moon, Brighton, & Callahan, 2002). A great deal of research supports the conclusion that gifted students need to use advanced materials and curricula if they are to reach their potential (Reis, Westberg, Kulikowich, & Purcell, 1998; VanTassel-Baska, 1995, 1998a).

Most educational settings do not adequately address and meet the needs of gifted students, and most teachers make only a few minor modifications to the curriculum when attempting to teach them (Archambault et al., 1993). Planning for 12 years of mathematics instruction for all students has sent many administrators and district curriculum specialists scrambling for the latest research on best practices, and the notion of meeting the needs of mathematically advanced students adds complexity to the task. The dilemma of choosing between acceleration to an advanced math class and providing planned enrichment activities within the regular classroom setting plagues math coordinators, curriculum specialists, superintendents, and parents.

The Critical Role of Assessment

According to the Principles and Standards for School Mathematics (NCTM, 2000, p. 23), assessment and instruction should be integrated so that assessment provides information for the teacher to use in making instructional decisions. Children who demonstrate high achievement in mathematics should be carefully evaluated to determine the extent of their talent and provide a profile of their strengths and weaknesses (Lupkowski-Shoplik, Sayler, & Assouline, 1994). Grade-level achievement test results can be somewhat helpful, for if a student scores extremely well, it may indicate that mathematics is an area of strength for him or her.

If a child scores at or above the 95th percentile on a grade-level achievement test, it is possible that the test did not have enough items of appropriate difficulty for the child, thus the score may not indicate his or her true level of understanding. In this case, it may be necessary to administer an above-grade-level test that will contain more items of higher difficulty. Julian Stanley pioneered this concept in 1971 when he began the talent searches (Stanley & Benbow, 1986), and 30 years of research have shown that out-of-level testing is a valuable tool for determining the level of programmatic modification needed for a gifted student.

Although a variety of standardized tests may be used for out-of-level testing, research has demonstrated the effectiveness of the EXPLORE test to identify talented elementary school students (Colangelo, Assouline, & Lu, 1994; Rotigel, 2000; Rotigel & Lupkowski-Shoplik, 1999). The EXPLORE (American College Testing Program, 1997) was developed for eighth-grade students and therefore contains a sufficient number of higher level items to allow students to demonstrate their proficiency more fully. According to ACT, the EXPLORE is directly related to student educational progress and includes a large number of complex problem-solving items and fewer measures of narrow skills. Many of the regional talent searches around the country offer EXPLORE testing in mathematics, as well as other subject areas.

No evaluation should be based simply on standardized testing, however. Teacher observations, classroom-based assessment, daily performance, and social and emotional needs must be included in the evaluation. It is important that data be gathered and analyzed by a multidisciplinary team of educators who are able to make and carry out educational recommendations for the student.

Program Evaluation and Curricular Collaboration

From the administrative perspective, a needs assessment could be conducted with all math teachers to determine each teacher's individual perceptions, teaching methods, and curricular successes or problems. An investigation of repeated topics, overlapping concepts, and ineffective activities could identify weaknesses in the math program. In order to meet students' needs, many concepts and topics in the curriculum could be compacted (Reis et al., 1998). For example, ratios and proportions could be coupled with simple fractional portions of sets. Some measurement or temperature concepts could be integrated into other curricular areas like science, thus allowing for more enrichment lessons in visual logic, inferential thinking, and deductive reasoning. According to VanTassel-Baska (1998b), efficient use of time is an important consideration in the development of talent.

Challenges for Teachers

Differentiation of Instruction

Once a sufficient foundation of information is gathered, an individualized plan can be established for each mathematically gifted student. It then becomes the responsibility of classroom teachers to implement the program. The plan may include enrichment experiences; differentiation of instruction, including pretesting and compacting the curriculum; flexible cluster grouping by topic or mathematics achievement; grade skipping in math; mentoring; and increased use of technology. The decision regarding which level of intervention is necessary should be based upon the evaluation. Highly gifted students may require more intense modifications such as grade skipping in mathematics. Rather than choosing one method over the other, research indicates that a combination of these approaches makes for a stronger program for divergent math thinkers (Stanley & Benbow, 1986). Daily ongoing assessment, teacher observations, achievement tests, and above-level testing can all be helpful in determining the type of program that will best meet the needs of each gifted child.

Defined by Tomlinson (1995), differentiated instruction is "the consistent use of a variety of instructional approaches to modify content, process, and/or products in response to the learning readiness and interest of academically diverse students." Teachers must add components to each lesson and modify the content for high-ability students, as well as for those who need remediation. For example, a lesson on calculating the area of polygons might include just the basic formula for most students, but should provide various real-world applications of calculating area for gifted learners. The increased complexity of the problems should require higher order thinking skills and provide opportunities for open-ended responses. Effective differentiation of instruction is very different from the unfortunate practice of simply assigning 20 problems to the gifted child while the remainder of the class is given only 10. "More of the same piled higher" is inappropriate and may lead children to conceal their abilities in order to avoid the extra, unnecessary work.

The task of differentiating each lesson requires accessing additional resources, planning for small-group interaction, and perhaps even modifying lessons during delivery (Tomlinson, 1995). In most instructional settings, the mathematical understanding and performance of the students is diverse, so classroom teachers plan their instruction with a myriad of learners and learning styles as the focus. Using a pretesting component in the math program allows for the identification of attained skills, strategies, and achieved concepts prior to the beginning of a new unit. For the gifted population, this helps eliminate the repetition from year to year in the mathematics curriculum. Pretesting and compacting the curriculum allows for a diagnostic approach for planning the teacher's instruction and allows educators to have a more accurate account of the skills and concepts students have mastered and those they have yet to be introduced to or need to strengthen. This process provides the foundation for effective differentiation of instruction, as each student should receive instruction based upon his or her identified instructional level (Howley, 2002). As noted by Winebrenner (2003), gifted students whose programs have been compacted can spend time working on their differentiated activities while their classmates are preparing for state assessments.

Enrichment and Grouping

It is certainly possible to meet the needs of some gifted students simply by enriching and modifying the existing mathematics curriculum. Enrichment is designed to expose students to a variety of topics related to those of the regular education program and to allow for further investigation of them.

In cases where math students are grouped according to their understanding of mathematical concepts and ideas, teachers can cover concepts at an appropriate pace for the group. Pretesting and compacting of the curriculum are helpful here, as they allow the group of mathematically talented students to be appropriately challenged. In addition, a classroom of homogeneously grouped gifted students would enable a teacher to apply the Enrichment Triad Model (Renzulli, 1977). For example, once students have mastered basic algebraic concepts, additional learning opportunities would be provided in the area of divergent thinking, individual projects, and group activities that would connect those algebraic concepts with real-world events and scenarios.

Acceleration and Technology

Since many mathematically talented students have already

mastered the basic skills, the enrichment activities and advanced projects their teachers have planned may not provide sufficient challenge. Indeed, for many talented youngsters, some degree of acceleration is needed based on their demonstrated achievement and ability. Simply working in the highest math class at their grade level may not meet gifted learners' needs, regardless of how well the teacher has differentiated the lessons. Gifted students may have already acquired the content and concepts presented in these classes, so acceleration to a math class at a higher grade level may be the most viable option. However, Lewis (2002) cautioned that acceleration should not be done unless it also meets the student's affective needs, which is sometimes difficult to determine.

It is important to match not only the mathematical content with the learner's needs, but also to provide an appropriate pace of instruction for his or her rate of acquisition, and acceleration may be the only way to accomplish this. Classroom experience and research demonstrate that, even though they may be younger, children who are exceptionally talented in mathematics will learn material much more quickly and with fewer repetitions than the regular curriculum allows (Sowell, 1993). Thus, the repetitions of a spiral curriculum become redundant and mundane to a gifted math student. On the other hand, gifted students in accelerated classes have opportunities to work with advanced concepts, in-depth topic investigations, and problems with real-world applicability.

Many advances in technology can assist the classroom teacher in meeting the learning needs of gifted math students by providing opportunities to explore complex problems and mathematical ideas (NCTM, 2000, p. 14). Readily accessible classroom computers, supervised access to the Internet, and appropriate software programs offer opportunities for gifted students to advance at their own rate.

A Conclusion That's Outside the Box

Teachers sometimes experience frustration when gifted children can arrive at correct answers through nontraditional methodologies or when some of their questions are far beyond the scope of the lesson at hand. Since gifted students can often interpret, predict, and analyze mathematical situations and problems better and faster than their teachers, a significantly different instructional approach may be necessary. Successful teachers of gifted learners adapt their teaching strategies to accommodate the students' unusual thinking strategies and methodologies. Unfortunately, inexperienced or untrained teachers sometimes make provisions for the gifted by assigning them enrichment worksheets, independent projects, or reports on famous mathematicians. Quantity, in this case, does not always equal quality (Greenes & Mode, 1999; Wolfle, 1986).

Being sensitive and aware of the unique characteristics of gifted students enables teachers to set more realistic expectations in the classroom. Teachers need to be confident in their own mathematical knowledge and teaching abilities in order to accept the divergent thinking abilities of their gifted students. In Mariah's case, traditional expectations of step-by-step problem solving with paper-and-pencil assignments may not be appropriate. When gifted students are able to arrive at the correct answer by following an unmarked thinking path, teachers should acknowledge this creative, divergent problem-solving strategy and not reprimand the student through missed points or a lowered grade because of not following more traditional techniques. Teachers should adapt the content where appropriate, condense the concepts where applicable, alter the pace of content acquisition, and allow for open-ended, multiple solutions to problems.

Meeting the needs of each learner is the goal of every teacher, and each grade level has its own unique challenges. Whether it is the preschooler, Bailey, who can often make math connections without formal instruction; Nathan, the third grader with the quirky thinking style; or Mariah, the prealgebra student who "sees" the answer without doing the work, each student thinks "outside the box." Accessing all available resources, using a variety of assessment tools, and choosing appropriate placements for each student are all aspects of meeting the individual needs of each learner. Being aware and sensitive to the unique characteristics of gifted learners will assist teachers in providing a myriad of opportunities for growth in mathematical reasoning and problem solving.

References

American College Testing Program (ACT). (1997). *EXPLORE technical manual.* Iowa City, IA: Author.

Archambault, F. X., Westberg, K. L., Brown, S. W., Hallmark, B. W., Emmons, C. L., & Zhang, W. (1993). *Regular classroom practices with gifted students: Results of a national survey of classroom teachers.* Storrs: National Research Center on the Gifted and Talented, University of Connecticut.

Colangelo, N., Assouline, S. G., & Lu, W. (1994). Using EXPLORE as an above-level instrument in the search for elementary student talent. In N. Colangelo, S. G. Assouline, & D. Ambroson (Eds.), *Talent development II: Proceedings from the 1993 H. B. and Jocelyn Wallace National Research Symposium on Talent Development* (pp. 281–297). Dayton: Ohio Psychology Press.

Greenes, C. (1981, February). Identifying the gifted student in mathematics. *Arithmetic Teacher,* 14–17.

Greenes, C., & Mode, M. (1999). Empowering teachers to discover, challenge, and support students with mathematical promise. In L. J. Sheffield (Ed.), *Developing mathematically promising students* (pp. 121–132). Reston, VA: National Council of Teachers of Mathematics.

Heid, M. K. (1983). Characteristics and special needs of the gifted student in mathematics. *Mathematics Teacher, 76,* 221–226.

Howley, A. (2002). The progress of gifted students in a rural district that emphasized acceleration strategies. *Roeper Review, 24,* 158–160.

Lewis, G. (2002). Alternatives to acceleration for the highly gifted child. *Roeper Review, 24,* 130–134.

Lupkowski-Shoplik, A. E., Sayler, M. F., & Assouline, S. G. (1994). Mathematics achievement of talented elementary students: Basic concepts vs. computation. In N. Colangelo, S. G. Assouline, & D. Ambroson (Eds.), *Talent development II: Proceedings from the 1993 Henry B. and Jocelyn Wallace National Research Symposium on Talent Development* (pp. 409–414). Dayton: Ohio Psychology Press.

Moon, T., Brighton, C., & Callahan, C. M. (2002). State standardized testing programs: Friend or foe of gifted education? *Roeper Review, 25,* 49–61.

National Council for Teachers of Mathematics (NCTM). (2000). *Principles and standards for school mathematics.* Reston, VA: Author.

Pletan, M. D., Robinson, N. M., Berninger, V. W., & Abbott, R.D. (1995). Parents' observations of kindergartners who are advanced in mathematical reasoning. *Journal for the Education of the Gifted, 19,* 30–44.

Reis, S. M., Westberg, K. L., Kulikowich, J. M., & Purcell, J. H. (1998). Curriculum compacting and achievement test scores: What does the research say? *Gifted Child Quarterly, 42*, 123–129.

Renzulli, J. (1977). *The enrichment triad model: A guide for developing defensible programs for the gifted and talented*. Mansfield Center, CT: Creative Learning Press.

Rotigel, J. V. (2000) *Exceptional mathematical talent: Comparing achievement in concepts and computation*. Unpublished doctoral dissertation, Indiana University of Pennsylvania.

Rotigel, J. V., & Lupkowski-Shoplik, A. (1999). Using talent searches to identify and meet the educational needs of mathematically talented youngsters. *School Science and Mathematics, 99*, 330–337.

Sheffield, L. J. (1994). *The development of gifted and talented mathematics students and the National Council of Teachers of Mathematics Standards* (Report No. RBDM 9404). Storrs: National Research Center on the Gifted and Talented, University of Connecticut. (ERIC Document Reproduction Service No. ED388011)

Sowell, E. J. (1993). Programs for mathematically gifted students: A review of empirical research. *Gifted Child Quarterly, 37*, 124–129.

Stanley, J. C., & Benbow, C. P. (1986). Youths who reason exceptionally well mathematically. In R. J. Sternberg & J. E. Davidson (Eds.), *Conceptions of giftedness* (pp. 362–387). New York: Cambridge University Press.

Tomlinson, C. A. (1995). Deciding to differentiate instruction in middle school: One school's journey. *Gifted Child Quarterly, 39*, 77–87.

VanTassel-Baska, J. (1995). The development of talent through curriculum. *Roeper Review, 18*, 98–102.

VanTassel-Baska, J. (1998a). *Excellence in educating gifted and talented learners* (3rd ed.). Denver: Love.

VanTassel-Baska, J. (1998b). The development of academic talent. *Phi Delta Kappan, 79*, 760–764.

Winebrenner, S. (2003). Teaching strategies for twice-exceptional students. *Intervention in School and Clinic, 38*, 131–137.

Wolfle, J. A. (1986). Enriching the mathematics program for middle school gifted students. *Roeper Review, 9*, 81–85.

Author Note

The authors would like to thank Michael Bosse and Jacquie Gentile for their helpful comments on an earlier version of this paper.

Helpful Web Sites

The following Web sites provide additional information regarding gifted students, their characteristics, and current research in the field. Administrators, teachers, parents, and paraprofessionals may find these sites worthwhile.

National Association for Gifted Children (NAGC)
http://www.nagc.org

Educators will benefit from the research, journals, conventions, and a nice collection of publications in the bookstore area.

American Association for Gifted Children (AAGC)
http://www.aagc.org

AAGC includes information that is especially helpful for parents and teachers of young gifted children.

National Research Center on the Gifted and Talented,
University of Connecticut
http://www.gifted.uconn.edu

Provides details on the Schoolwide Enrichment Model, graduate programs, and many resources.

Hoagies Gifted Education Page
http://www.hoagiesgifted.com

This extensive listing of conferences, resources of every kind, articles, and support for parents and teachers is a comprehensive "first stop" for everyone.

GT World
http://www.gtworld.org

GT World is designed primarily for parents and includes e-mail lists and lots of links to resources.

The following Web sites are designed for student use. The sites are easily accessible and provide information on math topics, problem-solving activities, and everyday mathematical applications. Students can explore a variety of mathematical concepts and strategies.

Math Forum
http://www.mathforum.org

Includes problems of the week and a teacher exchange.

A+ Math
http://www.aplusmath.com

This site for children includes a homework helper and math games.

GoMath
http://www.gomath.com

Students enjoy the automated math solutions and an SAT preparation area.

Mathlab
http://www.mathlab.com

A hands-on geometry site.

How Stuff Works
http://www.howstuffworks.com

A popular Web site for children that includes information on all sorts of topics.

The 24 Game
http://www.24game.com

An online opportunity for children of all ages to play The 24 Game.

chapter 2

Mathematically Gifted in the Heterogeneously Grouped Mathematics Classroom

what is a teacher to do?

by **Catherine Finlayson Reed**

*i*t is the first day of the new school year. I face many challenges as the teacher in this first-period class, a heterogeneously organized geometry class. Now in my 17th year of teaching mathematics, I am confident that I have sufficient education and experience to offer my students a rich and appropriately rigorous course. Today there are the usual "start-up" administrative activities and normal classroom management issues, and there are also issues of how best to assess the students' skills, how to adjust my presentations and expectations, and how to ascertain and incorporate students' preferred learning styles.

An additional teaching concern is represented by Adam, the student sitting at the front of the second row, arms folded across his chest, staring straight ahead. Around him, student voices buzz as other members of the class engage in small-group inquiry. Adam sits alone and waits. We both hear students challenging each other's answers and debating the relative merits of different problem-solving strategies, but Adam remains motionless, even when I approach his desk. In response to my "How's it going?," there is neither a flicker of an eyelid nor a change in his position.

If waiting is the game, I can outwait any adolescent. I stand quietly, attentive to the industry around me, but I don't move away from Adam. Finally, he pushes a sheet of binder paper toward me and points to a number written on it. When I neither move nor respond, Adam says, "The answer's 13." This is incorrect, but rather than tell him this, I ask, "How did you get that value?"

Without looking up, he tells me, "The work is so simple, any fool can see the answer." That is a loaded reply, as I suspect he knows. To tell him he is incorrect is to risk suggesting that he is a fool. To give him the correct answer is to grant him tacit permission to remain disengaged.

As with many mathematics students who have preceded Adam, I am witnessing some of the methods employed by a student who may be bright, bored, and underachieving, in spite of his incorrect answer. The immediate problem is finding a way to spark Adam's engagement. The larger problem is verifying Adam's ability and, if my assumption is correct, developing effective teaching strategies to meet the needs of this potentially high-end learner in a heterogeneously grouped mathematics classroom.

Heterogeneity

Schools face difficult decisions about the appropriate placement of students in mathematics classes (National Council of Teachers of Mathematics [NCTM], 2000). Although one of the educational goals for the United States was to be "first in the world in mathematics and science achievement by the year 2000" (Takahira, Gonzales, Frase, & Salganik, 1998, p. 17), the evidence from a variety of sources demonstrates that this goal has not been realized (Gonzales, Calsyn, Jocelyn, Mak, Kastberg, Arafeh, Williams, & Tsen, 2000; NCTM; Takahira et al.). Neither the practice of tracking nor that of heterogeneously grouping mathematics students has led to quantifiably higher standardized testing outcomes over the last decade.

Tracking, defined by Silver, Smith, and Nelson (1995) as placing middle and high school students in different mathematics classes based on ability, has led to unequal opportunities for students in the lower tracks to pursue higher level objectives. Students left out of the higher track courses are denied access to high-quality, challenging mathematics. Compared to students who understand and can do mathematics, these lower tracked students have diminished opportunities and options for shaping their futures (NCTM, 2000).

The heterogeneously grouped classroom presents a different set of challenges. Here, mathematics teachers work with students who evidence a wide range of abilities and prior knowledge (Mills, Ablard, & Gustin, 1994; VanTassel-Baska, 1991). The more variety exhibited by a group of students, the greater the potential challenge educators face in meeting their instructional needs. At what level should one teach in order to match curriculum with ability and build from prior knowledge?

Clark (1997) suggested that the optimal environment would be one where the level and pace of instruction is individually matched to each student. In reality, individual instruction is rarely possible in public school classrooms, where teachers usually work with large groups of students (Renzulli & Purcell, 1996). Teaching to the lower level of a class perpetuates the problem of low mathematics achievement, along with boredom and disengagement on the part of the middle and high-end learners. Teaching to the middle level causes the less-prepared students to struggle and fall farther behind, while the better prepared students, who remain unchallenged, lose their motivation to learn (Rimm & Lovance, 1992). Teaching to the high end also seems untenable, given the probable struggle and likely disengagement by less-prepared students.

Without changes in the level of classroom teaching, the outlook for promising mathematics students is bleak. According to Rimm and Lovance (1992), "if we don't provide a challenging environment, we are, in a *de facto* way, teaching our children to underachieve" (p. 10). Perhaps disengaged students like Adam are one result of the failure to teach at a level appropriate to high-end mathematics students, a failure that has been documented. Shore and Delcourt (1996) found "that when gifted children were heterogeneously grouped within classes, they received less than 20% of the teacher's attention and no curricular differentiation in 84% of their learning activities" (p. 142). They also reported that, "at best, only minor modifications to the regular curriculum were made for gifted students, even when there was a formal within-class gifted program in these schools" (p. 142).

Mathematical Giftedness

The basis for any discussion regarding teaching at a level appropriate for mathematically gifted students begins with a general understanding of giftedness before moving to a specific understanding of mathematical giftedness, which is difficult because there is no universally accepted definition of general giftedness (Gagné, 1995; Morelock, 1996; Sternberg, 1993).

This fundamental lack of agreement extends to mathematics, where differing descriptors of high mathematical performance and ability are evident in the literature (Sowell, 1993). Sowell, Zeigler, Bergwall, and Cartwright (1990) documented a variety of literature-based adjectives to describe exceptional mathematics students, including "promising," "high-end learners," "gifted and talented," and "academically superior." This multiplicity of descriptors within the specific domain of mathematics parallels the plurality of descriptors of giftedness in general.

Despite such different descriptions of mathematics students with high potential, the literature discussing these students (Sowell et al., 1990) agrees that they are able to do mathematics typically accomplished by older students or engage in qualitatively different mathematical thinking than their classmates or chronological peers. The literature also frames a picture of mathematical talent that corresponds to an understanding of giftedness as a dynamic and emerging trait. The NCTM Task Force on Mathematically Promising Students (Sheffield, 1999) recognized that mathematically gifted students come in all sizes, ages, and levels of academic achievement and noted that they may not possess identical traits. Furthermore, the task force avoided defining mathematical promise as giftedness. Instead, they defined mathematically promising students as "those who have the potential to become the leaders and problem solvers of the future" (Sheffield, p. 9).

The difficulties of the task force's definition of "mathematical promise" lie in recognizing and nurturing potential. Are mathematically promising students those who accurately solve demanding problems, those who do mathematics typically accomplished by older students, those who demonstrate both these characteristics, or those who evidence some other combination of mathematical attributes? Rather than debate whether mathematically promising students are gifted, for the purposes of this discussion, mathematical giftedness is regarded as an emerging promise or high ability with mathematics relative to one's peers. In addition, this discussion accepts that high-ability mathematics students may not demonstrate their abilities consistently. Over time, however, they exhibit clusters of classroom behaviors that are markedly different from their classmates.

Behaviors

Sowell, Zeigler, Bergwall, and Cartwright (1990) found that there are at least two types of mathematically gifted students. One type is the precocious student, able to do the mathematics typically accomplished by older students. The other type is the student who is able to solve demanding problems by employing qualitatively different thinking processes. Generally speaking, regardless of membership in either of these or other groups, highly able students acquire basic skills rapidly, reason quickly, and have the ability to form comprehensive generalizations more advanced than their agemates (Johnson, 1994).

While promising mathematics students will not evidence all of them, additional traits include longer attention spans, better memories, and greater persistence in wanting to find the solution to problems when compared to agemates (Garofalo, 1993). Some of these students may consistently create numerically inaccurate answers since they may spend relatively more time on the planning stages of problem solving and be less concerned about the accuracy of their calculations (Garofalo).

With no set of traits describing all high-end mathematics students, it is evident that no single method of instruction necessarily addresses the needs of these students. Since Clark's (1997) suggestion of individualizing instruction is untenable and the range of needs can be great in the heterogeneously grouped mathematics classroom, differentiation presents an attractive answer to the dilemma of what a teacher can do. Returning to Adam's geometry class illustrates the power of this method.

Differentiation

Adam was a student in one of the 17 heterogeneously grouped, nonhonors geometry classes in a large suburban high school. Twenty-two teachers formed the mathematics department, neither larger nor smaller than most mathematics departments in the more than two dozen high schools in this district. As part of one of the nation's largest school districts, Adam's school was experiencing the pressures that accompany explosive population growth. Already racially diverse, it was suffering from severe overcrowding. Classes were "capped" at 32, based on the size of the rooms. In reality, class sizes often grew above this cap. New students were entering the district on an average of 300 per week. They had to be assigned to schools and receive schedules. In Adam's class, the number of students exceeded and receded several times from the stated cap of 32.

Clearly, the needs of such a class were dynamic. At times, I needed to present new information to the class using direct instruction. At other times, I could maximize student focus and mastery by creating small groups for investigations, practice, or compacting materials new students needed to master. During these small-group sessions, I was able to move around the class, listening to student discussions, providing scaffolding, asking open-ended questions, and assessing progress. Structured appropriately, these group tasks met many of the NCTM (2000) recommendations for better mathematics teaching.

However, group work, per se, does not represent differentiation, even when students are working on different problems (Hoeflinger, 1998). For true differentiation to occur, the teacher should preassess understandings central to a unit and then purposefully modify activities to eliminate repetition and drill for those who already demonstrate mastery. These modifications fall into three general categories: (a) differentiated content, (b) differentiated process, and (c) differentiated product (Tomlinson, 1999).

The key components of modifications to the mathematics curriculum should attend to four broad principles: The teacher should (a) provide content with greater depth and higher complexity, (b) nurture a discovery approach that encourages students to explore concepts, (c) focus on providing complex open-ended problems, and (d) create opportunities for interdisciplinary connections (Stepanek, 1999).

Adam's class presented a full range of student abilities and interests. Two of the students qualified for Honors Geometry, but declined to take that accelerated course. As the year passed, I discovered another three whom I believed exhibited high mathematics potential. Three students were mainstreamed learning-disabled students with Individualized Education Plans (IEPs). Several students had barely passed Algebra, a prerequisite in this district for Geometry, so they struggled with the mathematics behind many of the year's units.

The adopted text was *Geometry: An Integrated Approach* (Larson, Boswell, & Stiff, 1995), which followed a standard sequence of geometric topics. After an overview of the subject, the text provided a review of basic algebra and reasoning skills. Immediately thereafter, the focus shifted to geometry, beginning with the study of triangles. I used the study of triangles as a foundational unit that carried classically important mathematics and served as a vehicle for differentiation experiences.

Over the course of the unit, I was able to provide three different types of differentiation: (a) extension, (b) open-ended investigation, and (c) self-selection of problems. Each type of differentiation provided an opportunity for content differentiation, process differentiation, and product differentiation.

Modification 1: Extension and Application

Adam's class began their study of triangles in October. The two major ideas that anchored the fall curriculum were congruency and the Pythagorean theorem. The class began the study of congruency by learning about the different kinds of triangles.

This required that they understand the descriptive attributes of triangles and correctly apply them. Adam and four other students grasped the descriptors of triangles, could apply them accurately, and needed more or different work in order to increase their mathematical understandings.

The initial modification presented to these five students was an extension of the task of defining and applying attributes to a group of shapes. Their task was to create at least two systems to describe and sort quadrilaterals. The students were to test their proposed systems, modify them as needed, and present their findings in two forms to the full class. They could work as one large group or as two small groups. No one could work alone.

My expectation was that these students would discuss and then organize all the quadrilateral shapes into two groups that paralleled the categorization of triangles by angle or length of side. Instead, they found the flaw in the assignment within moments of starting their considerations. Although they did not have the mathematical vocabulary, they discovered convex and concave quadrilaterals. After a lengthy debate among themselves and one short conference with me, they decided to include both types of quadrilaterals in their discussions because they wanted to be exhaustive in their considerations.

These students were ready to present their findings to the class before the rest of the students had reached a good place to stop their work. To allow these five to continue creating meaningful learning, I asked each of them to pose at least three questions about their new understandings. They were instructed to pool their questions, arrange them in a hierarchy from most to least important, write them on chart paper, post the papers to form an "inquiry wall," and begin researching the questions. Hypotheses or answers to these questions were added to the chart paper over the course of the next several months.

This wall became integral to the learning experience of the whole class. At different times during the fall semester, every member of the class contributed to the growing body of displayed information by adding questions, suggesting hypotheses, or providing answers. The wall became the foundation of self-selected, but focused, inquiry for the whole class during the fall semester.

Modification 2: Investigating an Open-Ended Question

As the class began to study the nature of congruency, Adam and two others from the first modification group immediately demonstrated an intuitive understanding of the pieces necessary to prove triangles congruent. Preassessment showed that another student not from the original five also understood. These four became a group that investigated the following open-ended question: What is the minimum information necessary to prove two triangles are congruent?

In pairs, the students proposed different ways to prove congruency. They tested the need to prove each of the ways they had identified. Then, the two pairs debated each other and sought counterexamples. They discovered that they could prove right triangle congruency with less information than they needed for all other triangles, and they discovered the ambiguous case that is usually held over until trigonometry. They demonstrated their new understandings by conferencing with me.

I posed one question that led to a presentation to the whole class: I asked the four if there was any idea they thought was interesting enough to share with their classmates. They thought the ambiguous case was "fun" and would clarify the common misconception that side-angle-angle proved congruency. They made a 15-minute presentation to the full class after the congruency unit test.

Modification 3: Self-Selection of Problems

The study of the Pythagorean theorem provided another opportunity for differentiation, this time for eight students. These students had easily mastered the application of the Pythagorean theorem, as well as the adaptations available for proving right triangle congruency. Not surprisingly, the strengths and interests of this larger group varied more than the strengths of the smaller groups.

To address this wider range of interests and needs, I allowed the students to self-select from a menu of opportunities. Their choices included exploring the history of the Pythagorean theorem; exploring at least three ways of proving the Pythagorean theorem; exploring different kinds of proofs, plus the difference between proof and demonstration; and exploring the nature of square roots, including how to visualize them. Those students who had selected the same topic worked together. Otherwise, a student worked alone. All were instructed to create some kind of poster or large visual, plus a short written explanation of their findings. They later presented these during a poster session held in conjunction with a series of research project presentations by the remaining members of the class.

Discussion of Modifications

These three modifications were linked to one long unit on triangles that I taught in the fall. Throughout the year, every unit presented additional points at which the same students demonstrated their readiness to move on to different material. At no time did I attempt to offer differentiation on a daily or task-by-task basis. Instead, I worked with the major concepts and skills that anchored each unit. Those who demonstrated mastery of these concepts and skills were invited to move into a differentiated option that was linked to the material being studied by the rest of the class.

The differentiation strategies employed in Adam's geometry class were not limited to a particular group of students (Stepanek, 1999). All students were eligible to participate in each modification based on demonstrated readiness. I prepared the modifications for points in the unit where I believed high-end students might become bored while their classmates worked more slowly. At these points in the units, all students were invited to demonstrate their understanding of the ideas fundamental to the concepts being developed and to show mastery of the skills necessary to perform the required calculations.

The class understood, based on the opportunity afforded each class member to demonstrate understanding and mastery, that I was not preselecting favored students for inclusion in some special group. The class also understood that the differentiation opportunities were not a pause from learning important mathematics. These differentiated opportunities became known with humor and a nod to Robert Frost as "The Road Not

Taken—By Most." Five students were ready for the first differentiated opportunity. Three of the first five plus two others participated in the second differentiated opportunity. The original five, the additional two from the second opportunity, and one other student demonstrated readiness for the third opportunity.

The advantages of the differentiated opportunities seemed to be understood by all. The high-end learners did not have to wait for their classmates before moving forward. They were able to work with more abstract material, such as the ambiguous case, and at a pace more aligned with their understandings. Yet, the varied presentations, posters, questions, hypotheses, evidence, and answers allowed all students to have access to the ideas that were considered by the small groups and individual investigators. Meanwhile, the other students progressed with their own learning, secure in the understanding that I was attentive to their needs. Each modification reflected Stepanek's (1999) ideas that differentiation should provide content with greater depth and higher complexity; nurture a discovery approach that encourages students to explore concepts; provide complex open-ended problems; and create opportunities for interdisciplinary connections.

Likewise, the modifications attended to content, process, and product differentiation (Tomlinson, 1999). Content differentiation occurred with each modification. When the students posed, sought, and answered their own questions during the first modification, they were creating their own content extensions. Later, as the next group discovered, investigated, and presented the ambiguous case to the class, they created their own content differentiation. They found the ambiguous case as a result of their open-ended explorations to establish the minimum information needed to prove triangle congruency.

The third modification provided the most variety and personal selection for the students. The four choices provided opportunities for abstraction, for the study of history and philosophic differences found in standards of evidence, and for concrete and tactile creations linking complex thought with real outcomes. The students chose from among the following: connecting with the history of a major topic in mathematics, considering different methods for proving the Pythagorean theorem, discovering the fundamental properties of proofs and contrasting these with the properties of demonstrations, and examining and seeking physical representations of radicals using geoboards.

Process differentiation occurred with all three modifications. Debate, conferencing, creating oral presentations and visual support materials, researching history, investigating the components necessary for proving theorems and conjectures, experimenting with ways to demonstrate irrational numbers (many radicals)—each of these provided the students with rich open-ended options from which they might create their own learning.

Product differentiation was also evident in each of the modifications. I required evidence of the students' new understandings for each modification. Sometimes, this evidence was oral, sometimes visual, and sometimes written. Each time, the whole class enjoyed hearing about the work these students had done, although the class was not required to develop the same level of understanding about the various topics as the investigators were.

Conclusions

The original question asked, "What's a teacher to do?" The heterogeneously grouped mathematics classroom presents a wide range of student interests and abilities. Attempting to teach to any single level in the class does not meet the needs of all students. Moving too slowly or with low-level material will not lead to any improvement in the aggregate mathematical abilities of students as measured by standardized tests or international research studies. Teaching to the high-end learners risks engaging in material too abstract or in pacing instruction too quickly for the majority of students. Regardless of the level at which we teach the whole class, we risk ignoring the needs of some portion of it. Differentiation provides a solution to the dilemma, a solution that can provide appropriate challenges at appropriate levels for all learners.

Differentiation is not an exclusionary tactic. As practiced in Adam's class, all students were eligible to participate in each modification. To meet the needs of all my students, I needed to assess their readiness to move on. The modifications provided differentiation for those who were ready to move ahead in their learning, but did not allow students to skip important conceptual understandings or skill acquisition. Instead, they underscored the importance of students continuing to learn important mathematics. The students who proved ready to move into a modification were responsible for respectful learning and were required to demonstrate their new understandings.

Taken together, the three modifications to the unit on triangles and the Pythagorean theorem attended to the four principles described by Stepanek (1999). The students who engaged in the modifications worked with content that had greater depth and complexity than the work assigned to the rest of the class and used a discovery approach that encouraged exploration. The topics provided complex open-ended problems. The third modification created specific opportunities for interdisciplinary connections.

What happened to Adam, the disengaged student we met at the start of this discussion? Did differentiation make a difference to his learning? I wish I could report that he became focused and excited about geometry in particular, mathematics in general, and learning for all time. He did not.

Although he qualified for all three of the modifications, he spent the entire year actively trying to remain disengaged. He argued that I was unfair to him when I expected him to learn materials that were different from those most of the class was studying. We conferenced about this point many times during the year, and each time Adam admitted that he already knew the material contained in the unit. Nevertheless, he would debate the rationale for being required to engage in new learning each time he demonstrated that he was ready to move forward into a modification.

Adam grudgingly participated in the first two modifications, and his work was excellent. He refused to select one of the options offered for the third differentiation. I would not assign one. His counselor and parents became involved at that point. Thereafter, he worked independently and well, creating an excellent product.

Based on the high level of his work and his yearlong resistance to the many opportunities to participate in differentiated learning, I concluded that the options Adam experienced with me in his ninth grade were too little, too late. Although he was capable of high-quality mathematics, he was content to remain disengaged and unchallenged. I will always wonder what might have occurred if Adam had encountered differentiated work much earlier in school.

References

Clark, B. (1997). Social ideologies and gifted education in today's schools. *Peabody Journal of Education, 72*, 81–100.

Gagné, F. (1995). From giftedness to talent: A developmental model and its impact on the language of the field. *Roeper Review 18*, 103–111.

Garofalo, J. (1993). Mathematical problem preferences of meaning-oriented and number-oriented problem solvers. *Journal for the Education of the Gifted, 17*, 26–40.

Gonzales, P., Calsyn, C., Jocelyn, L., Mak, K., Kastberg, D., Arafeh, S., Williams, T., & Tsen, W. (2000). *Pursuing excellence: Comparisons of international eighth-grade mathematics and science achievement from a U.S. perspective, 1995 and 1999.* Washington, DC: National Center for Education Statistics.

Hoeflinger, M. (1998). Mathematics and science in gifted education: Developing mathematically promising students. *Roeper Review, 20*, 244–247.

Johnson, D. T. (1994). Mathematics curriculum for the gifted. In J. VanTassel-Baska (Ed.), *Comprehensive curriculum for gifted learners* (pp. 231–261). Boston: Allyn and Bacon.

Larson, R. E., Boswell, L., & Stiff, L. (1995). *Geometry: An integrated approach.* Lexington, MA: D.C. Heath.

Mills, C. J., Ablard, K. E., & Gustin, W. C. (1994). Academically talented students' achievement in a flexibly paced mathematics program. *Journal for Research in Mathematics Education, 25*, 495–511.

Morelock, M. J. (1996). On the nature of giftedness and talent: Imposing order on chaos. *Roeper Review, 19*, 4–12.

National Council of Teachers of Mathematics (NCTM). (2000). *Principles and standards for school mathematics.* Reston, VA: Author.

Renzulli, J. S., & Purcell, J. H. (1996). Gifted education: A look around and a look ahead. *Roeper Review, 18*, 173–178.

Rimm, S. B., & Lovance, K. J. (1992). How acceleration may prevent underachievement syndrome. *Gifted Child Today, 15*(2), 9–14.

Sheffield, L. J. (Ed.). (1999). *Developing mathematically promising students.* Reston, VA: National Council of Teachers of Mathematics.

Shore, B. M., & Delcourt, M. A. B. (1996). Effective curricular and program practices in gifted education and the interface with general education. *Journal for the Education of the Gifted, 20*, 138–154.

Silver, E. A., Smith, M. S., & Nelson, B. S. (1995). The QUASAR project: Equity concerns meet mathematics education reform in the middle school. In W. G. Secada, E. Fennema, & L. B. Adajian (Eds.), *New directions for equity in mathematics education* (pp. 9–56). New York: Cambridge University Press.

Sowell, E. J. (1993). Programs for mathematically gifted students: A review of empirical research. *Gifted Child Quarterly, 37*, 124–132.

Sowell, E. J., Zeigler, A. J., Bergwall, L., & Cartwright, R. M. (1990). Identification and description of mathematically gifted students: A review of empirical research. *Gifted Child Quarterly, 34*, 147–154.

Stepanek, J. (1999). *The inclusive classroom. Meeting the needs of gifted students: Differentiating mathematics and science instruction.* Portland, OR: Northwest Regional Educational Lab. (ERIC Document Reproduction Service No. ED444306)

Sternberg, R. J. (1993). The concept of giftedness: A pentagonal implicit theory. In G. R. Block & K. Ackrill (Eds.), *The origins and development of high ability* (pp. 5–16). Chichester, England: Wiley.

Takahira, S., Gonzales, P., Frase, M., & Salganik, L.H. (1998). *Pursuing excellence: A study of U.S. twelfth-grade mathematics and science achievement in international context.* (USDE Publication No. NCES 98-049). Washington, DC: U.S. Government Printing Office. (ERIC Document Reproduction Service No. ED419717)

Tomlinson, C. A. (1999). *The differentiated classroom: Responding to the needs of all learners.* Alexandria, VA: Association for Supervision and Curriculum Development.

VanTassel-Baska, J. (1991). Gifted education in the balance: Building relationships with general education. *Gifted Child Quarterly, 35*, 20–25.

chapter 3

Catering for Mathematically Gifted Elementary Students

learning from challenging tasks

by **Carmel M. Diezmann** *and* **James J. Watters**

*b*oredom is a major concern of gifted students that stems from a lack of challenge in academic tasks and a perception by these students of the limited value of the learning experience (Feldhusen & Kroll, 1991; Galbraith, 1985; House, 1987). Academic tasks constitute the "work" of the classroom and ideally provide the necessary challenge that affords learning (Doyle, 1983, 1988). A key feature of challenging tasks is their authenticity within a domain. For example, an authentic mathematical task is characterized by its complexity, the obstacle to a readymade solution, and the need for high-level thinking and reasoning. Thus, challenging mathematical tasks for gifted students should be authentic tasks that provide opportunities for them to emulate the practices of mathematicians, though at a less sophisticated level. Gifted elementary students recognize the fundamental relationship between the level of a task's challenge and mathematical learning.

For example, in response to the question "Do you like your schoolwork easy or hard?," a gifted

12-year-old girl replied, "I like it hard so I can learn new things." She went on to say, "The perfect math lesson would be full of problems and hard questions."

Although mathematically gifted children are characterized by the quality of their reasoning (Johnson, 1983), these children require appropriate and challenging learning experiences to facilitate their cognitive development (Henningsen & Stein, 1997; Hoeflinger, 1998). It is unlikely that many classroom tasks that are selected for, or designed to suit, the majority of students in a heterogeneous class will be sufficiently challenging for gifted students. One response to this inherent lack of challenge in many classroom tasks is to supplement them with enrichment activities. For some gifted students, the level of challenge of enrichment tasks is still inadequate, and therefore more difficult work is required. Contrary to an intuitive reaction against providing students with very challenging work, there is evidence that gifted students crave such work:

> Figuratively, they [gifted students] were starved for mathematics at the proper pace and level and rejoiced in the opportunity to take it straight rather than being "enriched" with math puzzles, social studies discussions, trips to museums, critical thinking training not closely tied to mathematics, and so forth. (Stanley, 1991, p. 37)

Much has been written about instructional strategies and the pacing of content for the gifted, but less about the content itself (Shore & Delcourt, 1996; Tomlinson et. al, 1997; Willard-Holt, 1994). The purpose of this chapter is to develop a framework for enhancing the quality of mathematics learning in gifted children by considering the nature of the learning tasks and the teaching practices. Thus, we explore the suitability of the math content in a typical elementary mathematics task by analyzing the relationship between the level of the task's challenge and the learning opportunities that are provided for a gifted student. Additionally, the role of the teacher in monitoring and, where necessary, modifying the level of the task's challenge and in supporting a gifted student's learning is considered.

Theoretical Background

The Nature of the Learning Task

All learners require challenging tasks to facilitate learning and develop autonomy. To realize their potential, gifted students should engage in challenging tasks for three reasons related to cognition, metacognition, and motivation.

First, challenging tasks facilitate the development of *cognition* because they provide opportunities for students to develop mathematical power through high-level thinking and reasoning (Henningsen & Stein, 1997). Such tasks cater to preferences of mathematically gifted students for exploring patterns and relationships, producing holistic and lateral solutions, and working abstractly (House, 1987). Even at the elementary level, gifted students' capability and preference for working abstractly should be accommodated because the overuse of manipulatives can have a deleterious effect on mathematical ability (Marjoram, 1992).

Second, challenging tasks can encourage the use and development of *metacognitive skills*. Metacognition describes a person's knowledge and control of his or her cognitive functioning (Lester, Garofalo, & Kroll, 1989). Metacognitive performance is a crucial factor in high achievement (Schraw & Graham, 1997) that is necessary for success on challenging and novel tasks (Betts & Neihart, 1986). Specifically, success is influenced by knowing how to exploit useful knowledge (Schoenfeld, 1985) and knowing when to discontinue with inappropriate or unproductive strategies (Taplin, 1995). Polya (1945/1973) argued that metacognition facilitates the development of the type of knowledge that is of particular value for "future mathematicians":

> For him [the future mathematician], the most important part of his work is to look back at the completed solution. . . . He may find an unending variety of things to observe. He may meditate upon the difficulty of the problem and about the decisive idea; he may try to see what hampered him and what helped him finally. . . . He may compare and develop various methods. . . .

Digesting the problems he solved as completely as he can, he may acquire well-ordered knowledge, ready to use. (p. 205)

Third, solving challenging tasks enhances *motivation* (Lupkowski-Shoplik & Assouline, 1994). Challenge develops appropriate dispositions to learning, achievement (Bandura, Barbaranelli, Caprara, & Pastorelli, 1996), and intrinsic motivation (Vallerand, Gagné, Senécal, & Pelletier, 1994). Furthermore, the importance of success on challenging tasks develops self-efficacy and self-esteem (Bandura et al., 1996). Thus, motivation is a crucial component in the realization of giftedness and is a desirable goal for gifted education (Feldhusen & Hoover, 1986).

Challenging tasks facilitate the development of autonomy by capitalizing on students' cognitive and metacognitive abilities and motivation (Betts & Neihart, 1986). Autonomy is necessary for creativity in mathematics. To achieve autonomy, learning needs to be designed around rich and challenging problem situations that afford multiple opportunities for student construction of knowledge through inquiry, discussion, and argument (Palincsar, Magnusson, Marano, Ford, & Brown, 1997). Clearly challenging tasks are important for gifted students' learning, but equally important is the role of the teacher in providing appropriate tasks and supporting the students as they explore them.

The Role of the Teacher

The teacher has two key roles in supporting gifted students' learning. First, the teacher needs to select tasks that are appropriately challenging (Henningsen & Stein, 1997). If necessary, the teacher needs to moderate the difficulty of the tasks for particular students because the same task may not be of equivalent value for different students.

Second, to facilitate high-level cognition, the teacher needs to "proactively and consistently support students' cognitive activity without reducing the complexity and cognitive demand of the task" (Henningsen & Stein, 1997, p. 546). The teacher can provide extrinsic and intrinsic support to the students by engaging in the practice of cognitive apprenticeship, which is a suite of teaching strategies for developing expertise in domains such as mathematics (Collins, Brown, & Newman, 1989).

Extrinsic support is provided to the learners through scaffolding, modeling, and coaching. Of these strategies, scaffolding and modeling are key factors in facilitating high-level thinking and reasoning (Henningsen & Stein, 1997). Scaffolding is based on the notion that social interaction and expert guidance facilitate learning (Vygotsky, 1978). It bridges the gap between what a student can do independently and what he or she can do with support (Rosenshine & Meister, 1992); however, scaffolding is inherently temporary (Tobias, 1982). Scaffolds can be verbal cues, prompts, or hints (Rosenshine & Meister). Modeling is a form of scaffolding (Rosenshine & Meister) that provides students with a demonstration of the thought processes of an "expert" (Collins et al., 1989). Through cognitive modeling, the teacher "exposes learners to the teacher's ways of processing information by reasoning aloud while performing the procedures involved in a task" (Gorrell & Capron, 1990, p. 15).

Intrinsic support is provided by the teacher facilitating the processes of exploration and reflection on ideas and by scaffolding the learner's construction of meaning (Collins et al., 1989; Henningsen & Stein, 1997). However, the teacher needs to monitor and respond to the capability of the learner in order to maintain the challenge of the task (Palincsar & Brown, 1984). Listening plays a key role in monitoring and understanding students' thinking. However, the teacher needs to engage in interpretive, rather than evaluative, listening. Interpretive listening leads to dialogue or questioning that is information-seeking, with the teacher facilitating knowledge construction by probing responses, paraphrasing, providing opportunities for vocalization, and monitoring understanding (Davis, 1997). Interpretative listening implies that the teacher needs to be flexible and responsive to the student in implementing tasks.

The following example explores the level of challenge and the learning opportunities that a series of mathematical tasks provided for a mathematically gifted elementary student. This example highlights the role played by the teacher. Student-teacher interaction was crucial in responding to the capability of the learner and scaffolding the student to extend her achievement.

Example

Comparing the Value of Mathematical Tasks

Ten-year-old Michelle completed three tasks. The first task was a novel problem that similarly aged students found challenging (Diezmann, 1999):

At a party, five people met for the first time. They all shook hands with each other once. How many handshakes were there altogether?

Michelle spontaneously solved this task rapidly and with ease. Her solution involved drawing a simple diagram and summing the numbers from 1 to 4 (see Figure 3.1). Her rapid and successful response suggests that this task was easy for her. Although this task would have been sufficiently challenging for some 10-year-olds, for Michelle, it was unchallenging and, hence, of limited value for mathematical learning.

After her ready success on the first task, Michelle was asked to calculate the number of handshakes for six people (Task 2). The number of people was increased in an attempt to make the task more challenging. Michelle also completed this task rapidly and was again successful (see Figure 3.2). Thus, a slight increase in the size of the numbers was not sufficient to increase the cognitive challenge of this task for Michelle.

Michelle was then presented with a further variation on the initial task. She was asked to work out how many handshakes there would be if 100 people each shook hands with one another (Task 3). Though she had used the same method for the first two tasks (see Figure 3.1 and Figure 3.2), she immediately dismissed her previous method as inappropriate for the third task because it would involve a lengthy computation. Hence, this latter task had evoked a metacognitive response.

Despite her previous successes, Michelle was initially unable to proceed with the third task. In response to Michelle's difficulty, the teacher provided scaffolding in the form of hints and cues to enable Michelle to proceed. For example, when Michelle was puzzled about how to add the numbers from 1 to 99 efficiently, she was reminded about the visual representation

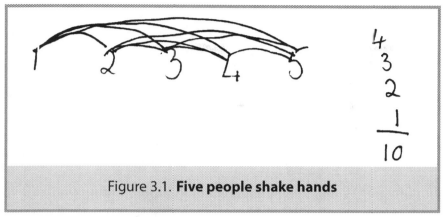

Figure 3.1. **Five people shake hands**

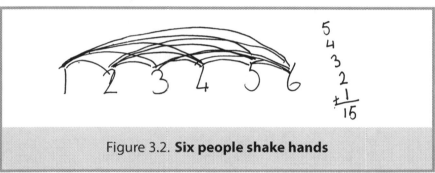

Figure 3.2. **Six people shake hands**

referred to as "rainbow tens." This representation is commonly used for learning the addition number facts to 10 (Department of Education, Queensland, 1991). The "rainbow tens" presents an analogous additive situation to Michelle's addition task, albeit with smaller numbers. Using analogies is a helpful problem-solving strategy (Polya, 1945/1973). After the hint to think about the "rainbow tens," Michelle subsequently drew this representation (see Figure 3.3). Her diagram shows how the numbers from 0 to 10 can be arranged in pairs so that each pair totals 10.

The "rainbow tens" representation provided Michelle with a means of conceptualizing how to add the numbers from 1 to 99 by making repeated combinations of 100 (e.g., 99 + 1; 98 + 2). The teacher then provided further hints to Michelle about how to represent and calculate all the sums of 100 that would be formed. Subsequently, Michelle calculated the answer to the handshake problem from the number of multiples of 100 (see

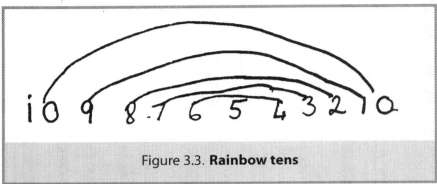

Figure 3.3. **Rainbow tens**

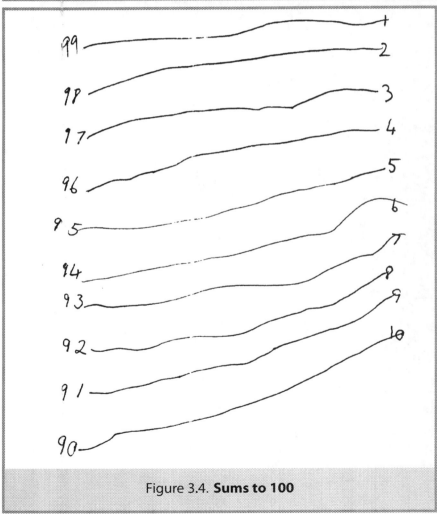

Figure 3.4. **Sums to 100**

Figure 3.4) and by subtracting 50 so it was not used twice in the calculation (see Figure 3.5).

The change in the number of handshakes from the second to third tasks (from 6 to 100) resulted in a substantial increase in the cognitive challenge of the task for Michelle. While she immediately recognized that her previous strategy would be inefficient for this task, due to the larger number of handshakes, she could not easily identify an alternative strategy. Although Michelle was unable to proceed with the task independently, she was able to proceed with the task with scaffolding. Thus, during this task, Michelle was working at the optimal level for learning. Support from the teacher enabled her to engage in an exploration of patterns and

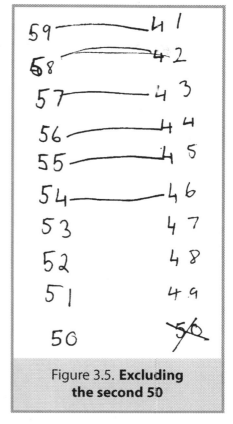

Figure 3.5. **Excluding the second 50**

relationships in determining how to sum the numbers to 99 and to explore a range of solution paths. Thus, a consequence of optimizing the cognitive challenge of this task for Michelle was that she was engaged in working mathematically, which involved using mathematical concepts and procedures, representations, rules, and reasoning (Greeno, 1994).

Although Michelle found the third task more challenging than the other tasks, she expressed a preference for this task, stating that it was more "interesting" than the others. Thus, the final task had motivational advantages in addition to providing Michelle with an opportunity to employ metacognitive skills.

Although the final task was sufficiently challenging for Michelle, when the 18th-century German mathematician Karl Gauss was 10 years old and was given the similar task of adding the integers from 1 to 100, he produced "an ingenious and instantaneous solution [and stated that] . . . there are 50 sums of 101" (Johnson, 1994, p. 244). Gauss' response to this task highlights the importance of considering the relative cognitive value of mathematical tasks for particular individuals.

Conclusion

Mathematical tasks that facilitate learning should be commensurate with the capability of the learner. For gifted students, this requires flexibility in the nature of the task and appropriate support from others. Tasks of sufficient difficulty need to be carefully chosen or existing classroom tasks need to be adapted, that is, "problematized."

In the handshake tasks discussed earlier, it was necessary for the task to be modified by the teacher before it became a sufficient challenge for Michelle. However, once the task was appropriately challenging, the teacher needed to provide support for her. The need for support should be viewed positively, rather than negatively, because the more complex task provides an opportunity for mathematical learning that is not provided by an easier task. Furthermore, the teacher provides feedback to the student, highlights successful strategies, and acknowledges her capability. Peers may also provide support and feedback.

Appropriate time allocation for tasks is also an important consideration. Gifted students achieve mastery faster and generally have more lengthy concentration spans than nongifted students (House, 1987). However, engaging in challenging tasks is time-consuming. Time is also required for the incubation of ideas, which is associated with insight into challenging problems (Boden, 1990). Thus, an effective goal should be that gifted students do fewer and more complex tasks over a longer period of time.

Problematizing tasks for gifted students is important to implement beyond the regular classroom and needs to be incorporated into curriculum differentiation practices such as acceleration (e.g., Stanley, 1991) and enrichment programs (e.g., Lupkowski-Shoplik & Assouline, 1994; Parker, 1989). However, if the tasks are inappropriate, the anticipated benefit will not be realized. For example, enrichment can be problematic if it consists of tasks related to irrelevant topics or "busywork" that lack challenge (House, 1987; Stanley; Worcester, 1979). However, acceleration can be equally problematic if the selection of academic tasks does not provide for the development of a comprehensive understanding of mathematics and, consequently, there are gaps in students' foundational mathematical knowledge (Lupkowski-Shoplik & Assouline). Thus, understanding the contribution of academic tasks to learning and achievement is critical in effective curriculum differentiation for gifted students.

Clearly challenging tasks are essential for effective mathematical learning. Gifted students stand to benefit when the academic tasks are appropriately challenging and the conditions for learning are optimized. This position has also been advocated by the National Council of Teachers of Mathematics (NCTM), which argues that these students "have a right to experience education as a relevant, challenging, and engaging enterprise" (House, 1987, p. 18). The NCTM has reiterated their advocacy for gifted students through their goal of "equity and excellence" in mathematics education (NCTM, 1998).

References

Bandura, A., Barbaranelli, C., Caprara, G. V., & Pastorelli, C. (1996). Multifaceted impact of self-efficacy beliefs on academic functioning. *Child Development, 67*, 1206–1222.

Betts, G. T., & Neihart, M. (1986). Implementing self-directed learning models for the gifted and talented. *Gifted Child Quarterly, 30*, 174–177.

Boden, M. (1990). *The creative mind: Myths and mechanisms.* London: Cardinal.

Collins, A., Brown, J. S., & Newman, S. E. (1989). Cognitive apprenticeship: Teaching the crafts of reading, writing, and mathematics. In L. B. Resnick, *Knowing, learning, and instruction: Essays in honor of Robert Glaser* (pp. 453–494). Hillsdale, NJ: Erlbaum.

Davis, B. (1997). Listening for differences: An evolving conception of mathematics teaching. *Journal for Research in Mathematics Education, 26*, 355–376.

Department of Education, Queensland. (1991). *Years 1–10 mathematics sourcebook: Year 3.* Brisbane, Queensland, Australia: Government Printer.

Diezmann, C. M. (1999). *The effect of instruction on children's use of diagrams in novel problem solving.* Unpublished doctoral dissertation, Queensland University of Technology, Australia.

Doyle, W. (1983). Academic work. *Review of Educational Research, 53,* 159–199.

Doyle, W. (1988). Work in mathematics classes: The context of students' thinking during instruction. *Educational Psychologist, 23,* 167–180.

Feldhusen, J. F., & Hoover, S. M. (1986). A conception of giftedness: Intelligence, self-concept, and motivation. *Roeper Review, 8,* 140–143.

Feldhusen, J. F., & Kroll, M. D. (1991). Boredom or challenge for the academically talented in school. *Gifted Education International, 7,* 80–81.

Galbraith, J. (1985). The eight great gripes of gifted kids: Responding to special needs. *Roeper Review, 8,* 15–18.

Gorrell, J., & Capron, E. (1990). Cognitive modeling and self-efficacy: Effects on preservice teachers' learning of teaching strategies. *Journal of Teacher Education, 41*(4), 15–22.

Greeno, J. G. (1994). Some further observations of the environment/model metaphor. *Journal for Research in Mathematics Education, 25,* 94–99.

Henningsen, M., & Stein, M. K. (1997). Mathematical tasks and student cognition: Classroom-based factors that support and inhibit high-level mathematical thinking and reasoning. *Journal for Research in Mathematics Education, 28,* 524–549.

Hoeflinger, M. (1998). Developing mathematically promising students. *Roeper Review, 20,* 244–247.

House, P. (Ed.) (1987). *Providing opportunities for the mathematically gifted K–12.* Reston, VA: National Council of Teachers of Mathematics.

Johnson, D. T. (1994). Mathematics curriculum for the gifted. In J. VanTassel-Baska (Ed.), *Comprehensive curriculum for gifted learners* (2nd ed., pp. 231–261). Boston: Allyn and Bacon.

Johnson, M. L. (1983). Identifying and teaching mathematically gifted elementary school students. *Arithmetic Teacher, 30*(5), 25–26.

Lester, F. K., Garofalo, J., & Kroll, D. L. (1989). *The role of metacognition in problem solving: A study of two grade seven classes.* (ERIC Document Reproduction Service No. ED314255)

Lupkowski-Shoplik, A. E., & Assouline, S. G. (1994). Evidence of extreme mathematical precocity: Case studies of talented youths. *Roeper Review, 16,* 144–151.

Marjoram, D. T. E. (1992). Teaching able mathematicians in school. *Gifted Education International 8*, 40–43.

National Council of Teachers of Mathematics (NCTM). (1998). *Principles and standards for school mathematics.* Reston, VA: Author.

Palincsar, A. S., & Brown, A. L. (1984). Reciprocal teaching of comprehension-fostering and comprehension monitoring activities. *Cognition and Instruction, 2,* 117–175.

Palincsar, A. S., Magnusson, S. J., Marano, N. L., Ford, D., & Brown, N. (1997, March). *Design principles informing and emerging from a community of practice.* Paper presented at the annual meeting of the American Educational Research Association, Chicago.

Parker, J. P. (1989). *Instructional strategies for teaching the gifted.* Boston: Allyn and Bacon.

Polya, G. (1973). *How to solve it: A new aspect of mathematical method* (2nd ed.). Princeton, NJ: Princeton University Press. (Original work published 1945)

Rosenshine, B., & Meister, C. (1992). The use of scaffolds for teaching higher-level cognitive strategies. *Educational Leadership, 49*(7), 26–33.

Schoenfeld, A. H. (1985). *Mathematical problem solving.* Orlando, FL: Academic Press.

Schraw, G., & Graham, T. (1997). Helping students develop metacognitive awareness. *Roeper Review, 20,* 4–8.

Shore, B. M., & Delcourt, M. A. B. (1996). Effective curricular and program practices in gifted education and the interface with general education. *Journal for the Education of the Gifted, 20,* 138–154.

Stanley, J. S. (1991). An academic model for educating the mathematically talented. *Gifted Child Quarterly, 35,* 36–42.

Taplin, M. (1995). An exploration of persevering students' management of problem solving strategies. *Focus on Learning Problems in Mathematics, 17*(1), 49–63.

Tobias, S. (1982). When do instructional methods make a difference? *Educational Researcher, 11,* 4–10.

Tomlinson, C. A., Callahan, C. M., Tomchin, E. M., Eiss, N., Imbeau, M., & Landrum, M. (1997). Becoming architects of communities of learning: Addressing academic diversity in contemporary classrooms. *Exceptional Children, 63,* 269–282.

Vallerand, R. J., Gagné, F., Senécal, C., & Pelletier, L. G. (1994). A comparison of the school intrinsic motivation and perceived competence of gifted and regular students. *Gifted Child Quarterly, 38,* 172–175.

Vygotsky, L. S. (1978). *Mind in society: The development of higher psychological processes.* Cambridge, England: Cambridge University Press.

Willard-Holt, C. (1994). Strategies for individualizing instruction in regular classrooms. *Roeper Review, 17,* 43–45.

Worcester, D. (1979). Enrichment. In W. George, S. Cohen, & J. Stanley (Eds.), *Educating the gifted: Acceleration and enrichment* (pp. 98–104). Baltimore, MD: Johns Hopkins University Press.

Instructional Strategies for Teaching Mathematically Gifted Students

chapter 4

Tiered Lessons

one way to differentiate mathematics instruction

by **Rebecca L. Pierce** *and* **Cheryll M. Adams**

he movement toward inclusion has impacted class-rooms by requiring teachers to respond to a broader range of academic needs. How can we possibly reach all the students in our classrooms when they are academically diverse, have special needs, are English as a Second Language (ESL) learners, or have some combination of any or all of these factors?

An answer to this question lies in differentiating instruction. Working in the Burris Laboratory School, an inclusion school using a resource consultation model to serve the needs of all its students, we have found that using tiered lessons is a viable method for differentiating instruction.

What is Differentiation?

Although differentiated instruction is not a new idea, the differentiation movement has recently taken center stage as a means of meeting the needs of all students in the classroom. It is an organized, yet flexible way of proactively adjusting teaching and learning to meet students where they are and help all students achieve maximum growth as learners (Tomlinson, 1999). Instruction may be differentiated in content/input, process/ sense-making, or product/output according to the students' readiness, interest, or learning style. By *content*, we mean the material that is being presented. *Process* activities help students practice or make sense out of the content, while *product* refers to the outcome of the lesson or unit, such as a test, project, or paper. *Readiness* refers to prior knowledge and a student's current skill and proficiency with the material presented in the lesson. A student's interest may be assessed with an interest inventory for the particular topic being studied or by an individual conversation with the student.

Essential elements for successful differentiation include (a) specific classroom-management techniques that address the special needs of a differentiated classroom; (b) planned use of anchoring activities; and (c) flexible use of time, space, and student groups. In a differentiated classroom, the management plan must include rules for working in a variety of configurations. You can only work with one group or individual at a time.

Therefore, we have developed two critical rules that thwart chaos and preserve sanity. The first is "Use 6-inch voices," meaning that students should modulate their speaking level so that their voices can only be heard 6 inches away. The second rule is "Ask three before me." If students need assistance completing a task or come to a stumbling block in a lesson and you are not available, they should find three other students to ask before they may interrupt you. If their three peers cannot answer the question, the student has permission to interrupt you. Adding the caveat that the student should also bring along the three students who were asked will nearly eliminate the chance that you will be interrupted except in extreme cases. Anchoring or "sponge" activities are provided for students to use when they are waiting for you to assist them before they can go any further or at the beginning of the class period to get them ready to work. A wide variety of materials and resources can serve as anchoring activities (see our Web site at http://www. bsu.edu/gate for a listing of books that have great activities for anchoring).

Flexible grouping arrangements such as pairs, triads, or quads, as well as whole-group and small-group instruction, create opportunities to meet individual needs. A flexible use of time allows lessons to proceed to their natural conclusion, rather than being carried out in set blocks of time. The desks or tables should be arranged in such a way as to facilitate group work, as well as whole-class groupings that encourage sharing of ideas.

A variety of instructional strategies, including compacting, learning contracts, cubing, and tiered lessons, can be used to differentiate instruction (for a discussion of these and other strategies, see Gregory & Chapman, 2002; Heacox, 2002; Smutney, Walker, & Meckstroth, 1997; Tomlinson, 1999; Winebrenner, 1992). It makes sense to alert the administration and your students' parents that you will be trying some new strategies in the classroom in case there are questions.

The tenets of differentiated instruction support both the Equity Principle and the Teaching Principle of the Principles and Standards for School Mathematics (National Council of Teachers of Mathematics [NCTM], 2000). These principles direct us to select and adapt content and curricula to meet the interests, abilities, and learning styles of our students; recognize our students' diversity; and encourage them to reach their full potential in mathematics.

What is a Tiered Lesson?

Tomlinson (1999) described tiered lessons as "the meat and potatoes of differentiated instruction." A tiered lesson is a differentiation strategy that addresses a particular standard, key concept, and generalization, but allows several pathways for students to arrive at an understanding of these components based on their interests, readiness, or learning profiles.

A lesson tiered by readiness level implies that the teacher has a good understanding of the students' ability levels with respect to the lesson and has designed the tiers to meet those needs. Think of a wedding cake with tiers of varying sizes. Many examples of lessons tiered in readiness have three tiers: below grade level, at grade level, and above grade level. There is no rule that states there may only be three tiers, however. The number of tiers you use will depend on the range of ability levels in your own classroom since you are forming tiers based on your assessment of your students' abilities to handle the material particular to *this* lesson. Students are regrouped the next time you use tiering as a strategy. Hence, the idea of flexible, rather than static, groups is essential.

No matter how you choose to differentiate the lesson—readiness, interest, or learning profile—the number of groups per tier will vary, as will the number of students per tier. You are not looking to form groups of equal size. When you form groups based on the readiness needs of individual students, Tier I may have two groups of three students, Tier II five groups of four students, and Tier III may have one group of two students. When the lesson is tiered by interest or learning profile, the same guidelines apply for forming groups: Different tiers may have varying numbers of students. Even when students are already homogeneously grouped in classes by ability, there is still variance in their ability levels that must be addressed.

To take a closer look at the anatomy of a tiered lesson, we have included a mathematics lesson (see Figure 4.1) that was developed as part of the Javits Grant, Project GATE, a federally funded partnership between the Indianapolis Public Schools and Ball State University, both in Indiana. When developing a tiered lesson, we have found the eight steps described below useful.

1. *First, identify the grade level and subject for which you will write the lesson.* In this case, the grade level is first and the subject is mathematics.

2. *Second, identify the standard (national, state, district, etc.) you are targeting.* A common mistake for those just beginning to tier is to develop three great activities and then try to force-fit them into a tiered lesson. Start with the standard first. If you don't know where you are going, how will you know if you get there? The author of this lesson has selected the Content Standard "Number and Operations" of the NCTM's (2000) Principles and Standards for School Mathematics (pp. 78–88).

3. *Third, identify the key concept and generalization.* The key concept follows from the standard. Ask yourself, "What big idea

Subject:	Mathematics
Grade:	1
Standard:	Numbers and Operations
Key Concept:	Students understand and represent commonly used fractions such as 1/4 and 1/2.
Generalization:	Students will be able to illustrate how fractions represent part of a whole.
Background:	Fractions (halves/thirds) have been introduced and illustrated by the students with pictures. Materials: Paper circles, squares, rectangles, triangles
Tier I:	Using paper circles (pizza) and squares (sandwich), students in pairs determine how to share the food equally and illustrate by folding the paper. Have two pairs determine how they can share equally with four people. They can cut the parts and stack them to see if they match. Have the quad repeat the process for sharing a Reese's Peanut Butter Cup equally with three people.
Tier II:	Using paper circles (pizza) and squares (sandwich), have students in triads determine how to share the food equally and illustrate by folding the paper. Have two triads determine how they can share equally with six people. Have the group of six repeat the process for sharing a birthday cake with 12 people. In each case, they can cut the parts and stack to match. Have the group start with half a cake and divide equally for 3, 6, and 12 people.
Tier III:	Using paper rectangles (sandwiches) and triangles (slices of pie), have students in pairs determine how to share the food in three different ways to get two equal parts. Have them illustrate by folding the paper. Are there other different ways to divide each shape equally? How many ways are there? Have the pair determine which shapes—circles, squares, rectangles, triangles—are easier to divide evenly and illustrate why with a particular food of their choice.
Assessment:	As the students work, the teacher will circulate among the groups and note the children's abilities to divide materials into equal parts and to recognize and check for equal parts. Can children explain orally how many equal parts there are and demonstrate how they know the parts are equal? It is at the teacher's discretion to determine which children need more in-depth questioning to ascertain mastery of the concept.

Figure 4.1. **Tiered lesson in mathematics:**
Tiered in content according to readiness

am I targeting?" In this example, it is to understand and represent commonly used fractions. While there are many concepts that could be covered under the standard chosen, this lesson addresses only one. The generalization follows from the concept chosen. Ask, "What do I want the students to know at the end of the lesson, regardless of their placement in the tiers?" In this lesson, all students will develop their understanding of fractions as representing parts of a whole.

4. *Fourth, be sure students have the background necessary to be successful in the lesson.* What scaffolding is necessary? What must you have already covered or what must the student have already learned? Are there other skills that must be taught first? Before engaging in this lesson, students have been exposed to halves and thirds. Fractions (halves/thirds) have been introduced to the students, and they have illustrated them with pictures. There are several literature books that illustrate fractional parts using food that could be used to introduce the lesson.

5. *Fifth, determine in which part of the lesson (content, process, product) you will tier.* You may choose to tier the content (what you want the students to learn), the process (the way students make sense out of the content), or the product (the outcome at the end of a lesson, lesson set, or unit—often a project). When beginning to tier, we suggest that you only tier one of these three. Once you are comfortable with tiering, you might try to tier more than one part in the same lesson. This lesson is tiered in content.

6. *Sixth, determine the type of tiering you will do: readiness, interest, or learning profile.* Readiness is based on the ability levels of the students. Giving a pretest is a good way to assess readiness. Students' interest in a topic is generally gauged through an interest survey, while the learning profile may be determined through various learning style inventories. In this lesson, the author chose readiness.

7. *Seventh, based on your choices above, determine how many tiers you will need and develop the lesson.* When tiering

according to readiness, you may have three tiers: below grade level, at grade level, and above grade level. If you choose to tier in interest or learning profile, you may control the number of tiers by limiting choices or using only a few different learning styles. For this lesson, students are placed in one of three tiers based on their ability to work with halves and thirds as assessed by the teacher through observation.

Differentiation means doing something different—qualitatively different. Make sure you keep this in mind when tiering the lessons. Second, be sure that students are doing challenging, respectful, and developmentally appropriate work within each tier. In other words, no group should be given "busywork." We don't want one group doing blackline practice sheets and another doing a fabulous experiment.

Notice in this lesson that all three tiers are working on fractions. Students in each tier use paper shapes to divide. However, the activities for each tier in the sample lesson, beginning in Tier I and moving through Tier III, differ from concrete to abstract and from simple to complex, to use Tomlinson's Equalizer word pairs (Tomlinson, 1999).

8. *Finally, develop the assessment component to the lesson.* The assessment can be formative, summative, or a combination of both. You may use some means of recording observations of the various groups, such as flip cards or sticky notes. You could develop a rubric for each tier based on the particular product that is created. You may give a formal paper-and-pencil test. Whatever it is, choose your assessment based on your needs and your lesson design.

In this lesson, the teacher observes the students as they share their answers and jots down notes for a formative assessment of each student. For example, which child is struggling with the concept? Which child is moving rapidly and accurately through the material? Whose answers show more thought and insight? Answers to these and other questions will assist you in determining who needs reteaching and who is ready to go beyond the material presented. A formal assessment is not used here since the standards emphasize that students should have "informal experiences [with fractions] at this age to help develop a foundation for deeper learning in the higher grades" (NCTM, 2000, p. 83).

When this lesson was taught, the students were engaged during the entire lesson. The lesson was introduced by reading the book *Eating Fractions* (McMillan, 1991). Students were then placed in groups based on their level of readiness to interact with the content. Four students did not have a clear understanding of halves and thirds. They needed a more concrete activity and were placed in Tier I. Another 12 students could recognize halves and thirds and were ready to complete the Tier II activity. They were placed in four triads. Two students had in-depth knowledge of halves and thirds and were placed in Tier III. This pair worked at a more abstract level, and the questions they were asked required them to use different critical thinking skills than the other two groups. Tier I and Tier II students were provided with activities from the book *Fractions* (Watt, 2001) to use as anchoring activities if they finished early or were waiting for the teacher's assistance. The anchor for Tier III students was *Apple Fractions* (Pallotta, 2002), which introduced fifths through tenths.

The second sample lesson (see Figure 4.2) is tiered in process according to learning style. In this case, students are grouped heterogeneously based on one of two learning preferences: kinesthetic or visual. The same eight steps for tiering a lesson apply in this case. In the second lesson, notice that the activities are at relatively the same level of complexity. This would be the "layer cake" model as opposed to the "wedding cake" model used when tiering according to readiness.

Final Thoughts

Time, energy, and patience are required to learn to differentiate instruction effectively in an academically diverse classroom. In addition, you need administrative and peer support, as well as professional development over extended periods of time; therefore, don't expect to have a differentiated classroom by

Subject:	Mathematics
Grade:	3
Standard:	#5 Geometry and #6 Spatial Sense
Key Concept:	Students work with geometric shapes and develop spatial sense.
Generalization:	Students identify lines of symmetry of objects.
Background:	This would be the fourth or fifth lesson in a unit on geometry where the first few lessons have covered various geometric shapes, as well as slides, flips, turns, congruence, and symmetry.
Tier I:	Kinesthetic Learners Pairs of students use brightly colored paper to make several simple origami designs. Provide guidance when necessary. When students are finished, have them unfold the figure(s), find any congruent figures, and identify lines of symmetry. Students then share the origami figures and have classmates try to construct them.
Tier II:	Visual Learners Pairs of students work with pictures of items from nature, such as a butterfly, sunflower, rainbow, snowflake, or starfish. Students find any congruent figures and identify lines of symmetry for each item. Students color the pictures to help show the lines of symmetry. Students cut out the figures and have classmates find the lines of symmetry.
Assessment:	Use a summative assessment noting students' abilities to identify the congruent figures and lines of symmetry. Have each student reflect in writing about congruent figures and lines of symmetry. From a list of objects in the classroom, students will select an object and write about whether or not the object has congruent parts, lines of symmetry, or both and then explain why. The students could also include a drawing that illustrates the congruent parts, lines of symmetry, or both.

Figure 4.2. **Tiered lesson in mathematics:**
Tiered in process according to learning style

Monday morning. Start small: Choose a favorite lesson in your next unit and differentiate it according to the needs of your students. Seek the expertise of specialists such as special and gifted education coordinators, media specialists, and others with whom you can collaborate to improve instruction in the academically diverse classroom.

For more information on tiering, contact the Center for Gifted Studies and Talent Development, Ball State University (BSU) at (800) 842-4251. Two Web sites that provide good examples of tiered lessons are the Center for Gifted Studies and Talent Development at BSU as part of the Javits Grant, Project GATE, and the Indiana Department of Education Gifted and Talented Unit's Tiered Lesson Project, developed by Cheryll Adams, Felicia Dixon, and Rebecca Pierce and funded by the Indiana Department of Education (IDOE). For the BSU site, go to http://www.bsu.edu/gate. For the IDOE site, go to http://doe.state.in.us/exceptional/gt/resources.html.

References

Gregory, G. H., & Chapman, C. (2002). *Differentiated instructional strategies: One size doesn't fit all.* Thousand Oaks, CA: Corwin Press.

Heacox, D. (2002). *Differentiating instruction in the regular classroom.* Minneapolis, MN: Free Spirit.

McMillan, B. (1991). *Eating fractions.* New York: Scholastic.

National Council of Teachers of Mathematics (NCTM). (2000). *Principles and standards for school mathematics.* Reston, VA: Author.

Pallotta, J. (2002). *Apple fractions.* New York: Scholastic.

Smutney, J., Walker, S., & Meckstroth, E. (1997). *Teaching young gifted children in the regular classroom.* Minneapolis, MN: Free Spirit.

Tomlinson, C. A. (1999). *The differentiated classroom: Responding to the needs of all learners.* Alexandria, VA: Association for Supervision and Curriculum Development.

Watt, F. (2001). *Fractions.* New York: Scholastic.

Winebrenner, S. (1992). *Teaching gifted kids in the regular classroom.* Minneapolis, MN: Free Spirit.

Author Note

Research for this chapter was supported under the Javits Act Program (Grant R206A980067) as administered by the Office of Educational Research and Improvement, U.S. Department of Education. Grantees undertaking such projects are encouraged to express freely their professional judgment. This chapter, therefore, does not necessarily represent positions or policies of the government, and no official endorsement should be inferred.

chapter 5

Can Distance Learning Meet the Needs of Gifted Elementary Math Students?

by **Sylvia St. Cyr**

I remember how nervous I was when I accepted the position as the teacher for gifted students in our building. The task seemed overwhelming—meeting the needs of students who could think faster, harder, and smarter than any of our regular learners. What could I possibly do to impact the lives and learning for this new arrangement of students I was about to educate?

These questions kept me focused and flexible as I prepared for my first year of gifted instruction. The newly created program I would institute involved facilitating general pull-out instruction to a select group of third- through sixth-grade students, as well as mathematics inclusion/independent study services for our mathematically gifted students. Our elementary school, in a low to moderate income suburban setting, had about 400 students, of which 21 were eligible for pull-out services. The format for providing services to my pupils seemed appropriate and manageable until I was presented with the following scenario regarding one of my students.

The first thing I learned about "Ryan" was that he had been accelerated in mathematics for both his second- and third-grade years. Ryan had been visiting higher grade levels at the time mathematics instruction occurred, and, through this simple method, he had been content accelerated. This meant that Ryan, when I began working with him, had already completed the fourth-grade mathematics curriculum even though he was commencing this grade level. I was further informed that I needed to enrich Ryan's math learning because the district superintendent had decided we could no longer accelerate him. This decision was based on the straightforward fact that we were not in a position to transport him to the junior high school for seventh-grade instruction when he reached sixth grade.

As I had already mapped out Ryan's schedule for continued mathematics acceleration, I felt that this decision was a clear impediment for him. My initial concern about Ryan was how to construct a program that would allow him to repeat the fourth-grade curriculum and yet still be engaged and challenged. This was no small task, and not one I took lightly, but Ryan and I managed to modify his learning by increasing the independent study blocks. During our independent study time, we explored various patterns, such as the Fibonocci sequence; worked on complex mathematics problems; and reviewed for the sixth-grade state mathematics league competition. I am convinced that acceleration would have been the most appropriate alternative for Ryan; however, I also believe we rose to the challenge and completed this year with as much success as was allowed, given our parameters. Thereafter, Ryan was provided independent study and inclusion services for his fifth-grade term, which is the service provided for most of the mathematically gifted students in our building.

Surely one can imagine my surprise and relief when, at our district's gifted team meeting last spring, I was informed that Ryan would be mathematically accelerated during his sixth-grade tenure. I was notified that he needed to complete his sixth- *and* seventh-grade math program in our sixth-grade setting. Another challenge, no doubt! Our assistant superintendent recommended that Ryan take a distance learning mathematics course provided by a prominent university. This program had been specifically formulated to accommodate highly gifted elementary students. Ryan's fifth-grade scores confirmed our belief that he was functioning at a higher level than our other gifted students because he scored a perfect 150 on his Otis Lennon exams and had a 99th percentile rank complete battery score for his fifth-grade Stanford Achievement Test, as well as the highest rank possible on the TOMA (Test of Mathematical Ability) I administered to him.

I was impressed that our district had finally come to realize Ryan's needs could be better met. I was also incredibly relieved that a university would meet Ryan's mathematical needs and that I would have instructional support because Ryan was exhausting my expertise at an exponential rate.

Supporting Our Beliefs

Finding research to support our belief that Ryan should be math accelerated was not a problem. Gallagher and Gallagher (1994) expressed that

> perhaps the simplest program modification emerges from the recognition that gifted students are performing two, three, or more grades beyond their expected grade level on achievement tests. From this observation comes the conclusion that they should be given content that matches their level of attainment rather than their age. (pp. 99–100)

Clark (1997) explained that "however acceleration is implemented, it will result in student completion of formal schooling in less time than is usually required. . . . Research has been almost uniformly positive in its results" (p. 205). Furthermore, Clark listed the advantages of acceleration:

- It can be used in any school.
- Acceleration allows capable students to enter their careers sooner, resulting in more productivity.
- A larger portion of students who are accelerated in primary and secondary schools attend highly selective colleges than gifted students who are not.

- Accelerated students do as well as, or often better than, the older students in their classes do.
- There is less boredom and dissatisfaction for bright students (pp. 205–206).

Clark cautioned that "although acceleration should not be used as the total plan for a gifted program, the literature shows very few disadvantages to this provision when used on an individual basis" (p. 207).

Mackey (1994) claimed we must

> consider that certain acceleration options allow students to modify not only their place—the *level* at which they are learning—but also their pace—the *rate* at which they are learning. Strategies that allow for the ongoing adjustment of pace, such as continuous progress, self-paced instruction . . . ensure that students are not merely jumping ahead, but also are advancing at an optimal rate. (p. 3)

Benefits for acceleration, listed by Southern and Jones (1991), include:

- increased efficiency;
- increased effectiveness;
- recognition;
- increased time for careers;
- increased productivity;
- increased options for academic exploration;
- exposure of the student to a new group of peers; and
- administrative economy (pp. 9–10).

Is Technology a Tool for Acceleration?

It was clear to me that content acceleration was an appropriate choice for Ryan, but what did I know about distance learning programs for gifted students? How could we be sure that this was an appropriate tool to access Ryan's abilities? I wanted to be clear about what this program involved before presenting it to his parents.

I researched the program's Web site and discovered that each mathematical topic covered through the course was listed and that the list was wide-ranging. I was able to access a sample lesson through the Web site, and I felt that the topic was adequately introduced. I also wanted feedback from someone in a school setting who had used this program, so I e-mailed a professor who uses this program for mathematics acceleration in her school district. She cautioned me about the program and said that it was only effective for her students if provided as an at-home enrichment model. Our assistant superintendent was firm in his belief that this would take place in our building during Ryan's mathematics instruction period, which required me to move forward in my decision about whether instituting this distance learning program would be an appropriate service option for him.

It was challenging to find research that supported distance learning at an elementary level. Nugent (2001) stated that

> it is imperative that empirical research be conducted to affirm the efficacy of the integrated technology practices that are being incorporated into gifted classrooms. In order to justify the cost and labor required to maintain and upgrade the technology already in place in our nations' schools, decisions based on research must be made in order to determine effective and ineffective uses of technology. (p. 42)

Questions posed by Nugent included "Are curricula that incorporate technology producing higher student educational outcomes than those that do not?" (p. 43), along with the demand that "as educators, we must evaluate the effectiveness of the practices we implement in order to adapt and adjust those practices to better address the varied needs of our gifted students" (p. 43).

After considering these comments, I decided that Ryan's journey could become a case study for me so that I could determine the effectiveness of this particular program for elementary gifted mathematics students. I found that, in our field, just as Nugent (2001) had noted, we do not have a variety of research or documentation to evaluate the effectiveness, or ineffectiveness, of such programs in elementary settings. This would be an ideal opportunity for me to conduct a study on the process our district would undergo, along with Ryan's progress.

Standards as Guidelines

This case study would connect to the following standards recommended by the National Educational Technology Standards (NETS) for teachers:

I.   Technology operations and concepts: *Teachers demonstrate a sound understanding of technology operations and concepts.*
II. Planning and designing learning environments and experiments: *Teachers plan and design effective learning environments and experiences supported by technology.*
III. Teaching, learning, and the curriculum: *Teachers implement curriculum plans that include methods and strategies for applying technology to maximize student learning.*
IV. Assessment and evaluation: *Teachers apply technology to facilitate a variety of effective assessment and evaluation strategies.*
V.   Productivity and professional practice: *Teachers use technology to enhance their productivity and professional practice* (NETS, n.d., para. 3–7).

The following National Council of Teachers of Mathematics (NCTM) technology principle also supports the practices used to accelerate Ryan in mathematics: "Technology is essential in teaching and learning mathematics; it influences the mathematics that is taught and enhances students' learning" (NCTM, n.d., The Technology Principle section, para. 1).

The following recommendations for using technology were specified by the NCTM:

*   Every student should have access to an appropriate calculator.
*   Every mathematics teacher should have access to a computer with appropriate software and network connections for instructional and noninstructional tasks.

- Every mathematics classroom should have computers with Internet connections available at all times for demonstrations and students' use.
- Every school mathematics program should provide students and teachers access to computers and other appropriate technology for individual, small-group, and whole-class use, as needed, on a daily basis.

Curriculum development, evaluation, and revision must take into account the mathematical opportunities provided by instructional technology. When a curriculum is implemented, time and emphasis must be given to the use of technology to teach mathematics concepts, skills, and applications in the ways they are encountered in an age of ever increasing access to more-powerful technology. (NCTM, 2003, para. 4–5).

Getting Started

I constructed a recommendation form to use in our district to determine eligibility for this service, which validated why Ryan should be the forerunner for our new mathematics acceleration program (see Figure 5.1).

At a team meeting, our staff—comprised of the sixth-grade teachers, our counselor, principal, and myself—reviewed the completed mathematics acceleration recommendation form for Ryan. We agreed that, based on his demonstrated needs, we would proceed with Ryan's acceleration using the distance learning program. A meeting with Ryan and his parents further confirmed that this was a suitable decision. Ryan's parents were supportive of our recommendations, and they concurred that this would be a viable tool to accelerate Ryan's mathematics curriculum. We discussed the negative considerations, as well, including the notion that we had not previewed this program and that we would be embarking into unmapped territory. Ryan was excited about the prospect of trying something innovative, and he was ready to commit to the challenges we had discussed. At the end of the 2001–2002 school year, we had a clear vision of Ryan's sixth-grade mathematics curriculum for the following

Instructional Strategies for Teaching Mathematically Gifted Students

Name of Student: _____

Grade: _____ Homeroom Teacher: _____ Math Teacher: _____

Parents: _____

Student is identified as Superior Cognitive   Yes   No
(Continue only if "yes" is circled)

How and when was student identified?

Grade: _____ Test: _____ Score/s: _____

* *

Current and Past Math Grades

_____   Recommended

                                                             Yes   No

Student Proficiency Math Scores: Recommended
(List all Years and Off Grade Scores)

Year: _____   Score: _____   Yes   No

Year: _____   Score: _____   Yes   No

Year: _____   Score: _____   Yes   No

* *

Tests Administered for Acceleration Assessment

TOMA Score and Rating   Recommended

Score: _____
Date Administered: _____   Yes   No

Textbook Inventory Test (Current Grade Level)   Recommended

Score: _____   Grade: _____
Date Administered: _____   Yes   No

Textbook Inventory Test (Next Grade Level)   Recommended

Score: _____   Grade: _____
Date Administered: _____   Yes   No

* *

Student Works well independently (1 = low, 5 = high)   1   2   3   4   5

Ranked by: _____

Comments: _____

_____

_____

Math Teacher Recommendation	Yes	No
Accelerated Math Teacher Recommendation	Yes	No
Parent/s Recommendation	Yes	No
Gifted Specialist Recommendation	Yes	No
Psychologist Recommendation	Yes	No
Principal Recommendation	Yes	No

Effective Date of Acceleration: _____ *
*(Using District Acceleration Services Guidelines)

Review Date: _____

Comments: _____

_____

_____

Signatures

Student _____   Date:_____

Parent _____   Date:_____

Parent _____   Date:_____

Math Teacher _____   Date:_____

Accelerated Math Teacher _____   Date:_____

Gifted Specialist _____   Date:_____

Principal _____   Date:_____

Psychologist _____   Date:_____

Figure 5.1. **Reading Community Schools Mathematics Acceleration Checklist**

year. We also charted the path for his mathematics acceleration through high school (see Figure 5.2).

Ryan would start with a technology course the first week of school, would finish the fifth/sixth-grade segment by winter break, and would begin on the seventh-grade curriculum in January. He would then be in a position to enroll in an eighth-grade algebra class when he reached junior high school.

I registered Ryan for the program the third week in August. I was informed that I would be receiving CD-ROMs that had the entire program's content on them, and we would be ready to commence as soon as the discs arrived. We would be sending weekly e-mail reports of Ryan's progress and work to his tutor at the university, to whom Ryan would have access online. Ryan would also be able to access his own Web page on the Internet, which would provide him with data regarding his progress and standing.

The CD-ROMs arrived 1 week after school had started (Ryan was included in the regular sixth-grade math class during this time). I wasted no time in arranging to have our technology support person download the discs onto the terminal in my room. I was excited and eager to find out what our district funds of approximately $500 for each 3-month period had bought us. Ryan was also eager to embark on this innovative journey.

The first thing our technology specialist noticed when he tried to download the program onto my computer was a message that informed us the program was not compatible with Macintosh computers. I could not believe that we had overlooked this during the registration process. It was so frustrating to think that we had not considered the technical requirements as we were evaluating the program curriculum. What a ghastly oversight this was! I was now relying completely on the technology person, Terry, to problem-solve me out of this. Terry said that we could probably get a PC from somewhere. We notified my principal about our problem, and he agreed that we should try to locate a PC. Another district technology support person kindly offered to donate her PC for our purposes; however, we would have to wait until her husband had a chance to download everything from the hard drive. The waiting stretched out to 3 agonizing weeks. When the PC finally arrived in my classroom, Terry and I were filled with anticipation again.

Criteria

1. Student has been identified as Superior Cognitive according to Reading School District standards (127 or above S.A.I. and 95th percentile composite score on an achievement test).

2. Student is recommended by mathematics teacher and/or g fted specialist.

3. Parent(s) have been informed and have been interviewed by the designated building team.

4. Mathematics Acceleration Checklist, testing, and scoring are complete and specify acceleration recommendations.

5. Psychologist has interviewed student.

6. Written Education Plan and checklist forms are reviewed and signed by all participants at a final team meeting.

Services

• Mathematics Acceleration in grades 3, 4, and 5.
(Student participates in higher grade level mathematics sessions.)

• Student works on independent study projects and distance learning program for sixth-grade term and completes the seventh-grade curriculum through distance learning requirements.

• During junior/senior high school, the student will be accelerated as follows:

7th Grade	Algebra I
8th Grade	Geometry
9th Grade	Algebra II
10th Grade	Precalculus
11th Grade	Calculus and/or Discreet Mathematics
12th Grade	Postsecondary Mathematics course/s

Figure 5.2. **Reading Community Schools criteria and services for mathematically gifted students**

Terry spent at least 7 hours that Saturday and some time on Sunday trying to get past the first page of the program. When I checked in on that particular Sunday, I was thrilled to see the home page for the program on the PC in my room. I experienced the same thing Terry did when I tried to log on, however, as there was an obvious malfunction because we could not access the program beyond the opening screen.

For the sake of brevity, I will condense the process that ensued. I will only caution that it took more than 2 months to correct the problems. The solution required buying a Virtual PC program to place on a Macintosh computer. The cost for this was approximately $230. This also entailed numerous hours of labor for our technology person, who went through an arduous process of phone tag with the university. We received several different discs at various times throughout this process. The time zone factor made communication with the university impractical and nonproductive. I will forever be indebted to Terry for his work ethic, and I know we would not have been able to manage this without his dedication and expertise. In fairness to the university, however, it must be mentioned that an extension on Ryan's tuition was awarded due to our difficulties with achieving technical stability.

During the interim, Ryan's math program was modified once again. I decided to include him in the American Math Competition. Preparation for this, along with regular mathematics classroom participation, kept him challenged, but it was disappointing to know that we had let him down again. My credibility with him was being stretched, and there were certainly moments when I underwent feelings of failure for not having had enough foresight about the technological requirements for this program.

Finally Online

At 10:15 a.m. on November 7th Ryan was able to complete the first 20-minute lesson using the distance learning program. The course allowed me to input the grade level at which he would commence. I started Ryan at the beginning of the fifth-grade level because I felt we needed to understand the format and content before adjusting things to a higher level. I deemed it safer to wait and see how the concepts were presented before modifying this in any way.

The session started with a math racing game that involved dividing four-digit numbers by two-digit numbers. It was wonderful to see a variation of the traditional flash cards Ryan had been exposed to, which involved games of "Around the World" with math facts of one digit by one digit multiplication problems. Ryan loved competing with the computer. The program allowed him to choose a pace of slow, normal, or fast. I advised Ryan to start with slow, but his competitive nature compelled him to start with the normal setting. Ryan was accustomed to being the fastest and brightest student at all times, and he did not understand that this program was formulated for students who had even more capabilities than he did. After the first round at the normal level, Ryan realized that he would experience more success by choosing slow for his next race.

Ryan was extremely verbal while competing with the computer. He practically elevated himself out of his chair because he was enjoying the challenge so much. The final race he completed before beginning his first lesson showed a 95% accuracy along with a score of an average of 8.4 seconds to solve each of 24 problems. I appreciated the instant feedback about his scores. I already felt much better about the possibilities this might provide for him.

The next part of the session was a lesson that included improper fractions, pictographs, geometry, line graphs, bar graphs, renaming fractions, equalities and inequalities, and translating word problems into algebraic equations. The session took about 20 minutes to complete. Ryan's comments included, "This is good math. We don't do this much in our class" and "Okay. Good lecture" when the taped instructions of the professor had finished. Scores for this lesson were 62 problems correct and 3 incorrect. I did not want to accelerate Ryan's level just yet, but I felt that the feedback would give me a complete picture of how he was performing so that I could adjust and modify at any time, if need be.

Preliminary Conclusions

Ryan has been working with this program for several months now. I compiled a schedule for him that includes one or more sessions daily. Ryan completes these sessions in my room in a controlled setting. Although our original goal was to have him work on his sessions in his classroom during his mathematics instruction, after seeing the challenges Ryan has encountered, I believe he needs more accountability than the regular classroom allows. Ryan also enjoys verbally interacting with his learning, which would make him a distraction to his classmates. Furthermore, he should be carefully monitored because he does not always take the time required to understand new concepts unless he is monitored.

The program provides a score for each lesson and the ability to access homework for concepts covered. Also available is a section for teachers or parents that has helpful instructional suggestions. I find myself referring to this section frequently so that I can present these concepts to Ryan in the same manner he is being taught by the program. There have been several times when Ryan needed these verbal mini-lessons before he could understand a new concept. The curriculum moves at a very fast pace, always covering a wide variety of mathematical concepts, and each lesson begins with a mini-review lesson.

Ryan has not stopped verbalizing as he solves problems. He rarely uses scratch paper for the lessons. Although he is capable of solving almost every problem mentally, it does take him "think time" to get there. He has spent many moments rocking and frenetically moving about in his chair, which is the behavior he has historically exhibited when feeling challenged. It has been a pleasure watching him as he moves through the program, and I have been impressed with the caliber of material with which he is presented.

Ryan's parents were able to observe him completing a lesson during our conferences this fall. They, too, were impressed with the content and pace. The timing of Ryan's demonstration was perfect because we had just completed a conference regarding our next mathematically accelerated student, a third grader who would be completing the same distance learning program when he reached sixth grade. The student and his parents stayed to preview the program and watch Ryan complete the session. They were impressed that their son, who had been assessed using the newly created eligibility form (see Figure 5.1), would be partaking in this program, as well. This student's acceleration was a direct result of the foundation we had established through Ryan's process.

Ryan has been continuing his independent studies and is now working on the seventh-grade accelerated curriculum. He had trouble taking his sixth-grade exit exam, which required a score of at least 85% before he was able to commence the seventh-grade curriculum. He would hasten through the test and choose his answers randomly instead of spending the time needed to concentrate on each question. I was impressed when his tutor phoned him at home to discuss his test scores with him. She suggested that he take a written exam that she would fax to our school. Ryan scored 92% on this test, which was considerably higher than his computer-generated scores. This allowed him to advance to the seventh-grade accelerated curriculum in April.

Ryan is not going to complete this curriculum before the end of the year, but I was able to compare the curriculum at our junior high school with the various concepts being covered through the distance learning program, and, as I suspected, Ryan has already been exposed to more concepts through the distance learning program than the junior high students have covered in their textbooks. It was reassuring to know that this distance learning program would become a bridge for Ryan, and future qualified students, to the pathway of mathematical acceleration for the remainder of their tenure in our district.

This program is also helping me to understand better how to teach and reach gifted mathematics students. I try to listen to each lecture along with Ryan, and I always closely monitor the content so that I can stay abreast of his learning. He still weaves in and out of the regular sixth-grade mathematics instruction in his homeroom because he benefits from all mathematics-related learning and enjoys being with his classmates. He also seems to thrive on the affirmation he gets from being successful in a group setting.

Pitfalls with the distance learning program still prevail, including initial difficulty sending e-mail reports to the university. It took several months to establish a system of sending the e-mail reports and communicating with Ryan's tutor regularly. We now have a regular routine established, and Ryan has been utilizing this aspect of the service more appropriately, although he does need to be continually reminded to read these e-mails and review the information being transmitted by them. The information in these e-mails is extremely helpful because Ryan's tutor reviews any concepts he has struggled with during a session and presents them in a slightly different format than the lectures on the CD-ROM discs.

There have been some glitches in the system that I have not been able to work out. One example is the math race section that covers least common denominators. This section was improperly programmed because, upon entering the correct answer, the computer repeatedly marks it as incorrect. After explaining this through e-mail to Ryan's tutor, I was informed that I could turn the math races off. This was disappointing because Ryan had enjoyed the competitive challenge of increasing his accuracy and speed through these activities; however, the math race program would not move beyond the least common denominator section, so we found we had no choice but to disable this function.

When reviewing this experience overall, I can see that providing this type of service is extremely beneficial for students with strong mathematical abilities. Distance learning is an exciting and potent tool for the use of extending learning, and this particular program has been professionally structured and does a remarkable job of meeting the needs of high-level learners.

Final Thoughts

Wouldn't life be wonderful if we were always given second chances? As an educator, it is frightening to think of how often my learning curves have threatened the learning of my students. There is no way to recoup the opportunities that were taken from Ryan. Suffice to say he is laying the groundwork for other students who will follow in his footsteps.

What I have learned from this experience is to allow time for the unexpected when dealing with technology. I have further learned that you need a strong technological support system in your school to ensure that access can be restored. The physical setting for online learning is important, as well. Students need to have a place where they can respond to their learning. The regular classroom would not be the most appropriate environment for this type of independent study program. Funding must also be considered when dealing with distance learning programs. Finally, the small print—the kind that reads "System Requirements"—will always be the first piece of information I review before considering any type of technology program for my students!

The use of distance learning in an elementary setting has truly just begun. I realize now how important it is for educators to have a full understanding of what is available for their students through the use of technology and, more importantly, how to access what is available. I think professional development regarding technology in our field is only in the infant stages. We, as teachers, need to find the time and resources to become proficient in this vast field. My professional development plan will always include goals on how to improve my knowledge in this area. To ensure that my students are provided with everything they deserve in an educational setting, it is my responsibility to pursue and move forward with my own learning in this vast virtual realm that provides such rich possibilities for exploration.

Future Trends

Although data specific to distance learning programs for gifted elementary mathematics students was not available, the following information, obtained from the report *Virtual Schools: Trends and Issues* (Clark, 2001), suggests that further research needs to be conducted regarding distance learning in U.S. schools.

- Virtual K–12 education is a form of distance education.
- Virtual schools are defined as educational organizations that offer K–12 courses through Internet- or Web-based methods.
- The trend from virtual high schools to virtual K–12 schools continues.
- It was estimated that 40,000 to 50,000 K–12 students enrolled in an online course in 2001–2002.
- The most common tuition reported was $300 per semester, but prices varied greatly.
- Calculus AB was the online AP course offered by the most

schools.

- Almost 8 in 10 virtual schools indicated that they developed or codeveloped at least some of their own courses. Only about 12% of virtual schools said they relied entirely on external providers for their courses.

- At least 14 states have a planned or operational state-sanctioned, state-level virtual school in place. Other types of virtual school organizations include university-based virtual schools, virtual school consortia, virtual schools operated by schools and districts, virtual charter schools operated by state-chartered entities, and virtual schools operated by private school entities.

References

Clark, B. (1997). *Growing up gifted: Developing the potential of children at home and school* (5th ed.). Upper Saddle River, NJ: Prentice-Hall.

Clark, T. (2001). *Virtual schools: Trends and issues.* Retrieved May 16, 2003, from http://www.dlrn.org/virtualstudy.pdf

Gallagher, S., & Gallagher, J. (1994) *Teaching the gifted child* (5th ed.). Needham Heights, MA: Allyn and Bacon.

Mackey, L. (1994). *In the balance: Acceleration: Evaluating the controversy over higher-speed education.* Retrieved January 12, 2003, from http://www.jhu.edu/~gifted/pubres/accel.html

National Council of Teachers of Mathematics (NCTM). (1987). *Providing opportunities for the mathematically gifted K–12.* Reston, VA: Author.

National Council of Teachers of Mathematics (NCTM). (n.d.). *Overview of principles and standards for school mathematics.* Retrieved March 18, 2003, from http://www.nctm.org/standards/principles.htm

National Council of Teachers of Mathematics (NCTM). (2003). *The use of technology in the learning and teaching of mathematics.* Retrieved January 30, 2004, from http://www. nctm.org/about/use_of_technology.htm

National Educational Technology Standards (NETS). (n.d.). *Curriculum and content area standards: NETS for teachers.* Retrieved March 18, 2003, from http://cnets.iste.org/currstands/cstands-netst.html

Nugent, S. (2001). Technology and the gifted: Focus, facets, and the future. *Gifted Child Today, 24*(4), 38–45.

Southern, T., & Jones, E. (1991). *The academic acceleration of gifted children.* New York: Teachers College Press.

Appendix 1:
Distance Learning Programs for Gifted Elementary Students

Center for Talent
Development (CTD)
http://www.ctd.northwestern.edu

The LearningLinks Program (formerly LetterLinks) is designed for independent learning and offers students in fourth through 12th grades honors-level and Advanced Placement courses for high school credit. Northwestern University provides this program. The Web site lists other distance learning opportunities.

Center for Talented Youth (CTY)
http://www.jhu.edu/gifted/about

K-12 distance education programs through Johns Hopkins University provide academically challenging courses in writing, mathematics, computer science, and physics, guided by CTY tutors. Uses online and CD-ROM formats to enable students to take accelerated courses year-round at home or school.

Education Program
for Gifted Youth (EPGY)
http://www-epgy.Stanford.edu/overview/info.html

This program, provided by Stanford University, offers accelerated coursework for gifted students from kindergarten through high school. Presently, more than 3,000 students from around the world are enrolled in the EPGY program.

The Internet Academy
http://www.iacademy.org/IA/AboutIA/Welcome.html

The Internet Academy provides courses and teachers to students via the Internet. Washington State certified teachers provide instruction to students in grades K–12. The program allows for innovative uses of technology, customized learning environments, and access to skilled instructors (not specifically for gifted students).

The Gelfand Outreach Program in Mathematics (GOPM)

Rutgers University Center for Mathematics, Science, and Computer Education provides this program for middle and high school students. Students work at their own pace and enjoy the benefit of individual feedback from a GOPM mentor who reads all of the their work and provides individual responses. For further information, call (732) 445-3491 or e-mail gopm@math.rutgers.edu.

Virtual School for the Gifted (VSG)
http://www.vsg.edu.au

The VSG is an online school that specializes in providing enrichment courses to complement and extend the regular curriculum. The VSG works with schools and home schools to provide courses to challenge able students.

Appendix 2
Web Resources

The following Web sites have comprehensive lists of distance learning programs.

Hoagie's Gifted Education Page:
Distance Learning
http://www.hoagiesgifted.org/distance_learning.htm

Programs for students of all ages

Northwestern University Center
for Talent Development Resources
http://www.ctd.northwestern.edu:16080/resources

Programs for middle and high school students. This informative Web site includes a definition of distance learning, a list of the special characteristics required of the students, and recommendations for parents.

Yahoo! Directory:
Distance Learning K–12
http://dir.yahoo.com/Education/Distance_Learning/K_12

Courses listed are for all age ranges, but are not specifically for gifted students.

Virtual Schools: Trends and Issues:
A Study of Virtual Schools in the United States
http://www.wested.org/online_pubs/virtualschools.pdf

This study lists the trends for virtual schools and includes three pages of links to schools offering at least a partial K–12 curricula through Web-based courses. This document should be a starting point for educators and administrators considering Web-based instruction for their students. Included is an extensive list of recommendations, as well as survey results from participating virtual schools.

...natical Acceleration
...ixed-Ability Classroom

chapter 6

Mathematical Acceleration in a Mixed-Ability Classroom

applying a tiered-objectives model

by **Todd Kettler** *and* **Marc Curliss**

*W*hat does effective differentiation look like in a math classroom, and in particular, what does it look like in a mixed-ability math classroom? Those essential questions must be confronted by teachers and program directors who work with gifted and talented students in the field of mathematics. Once a commitment is made, it is not acceptable for students with high abilities in math to traverse lethargically the terrain of the mathematics curriculum. Educators of the gifted and talented must confront the best practices and ask, "How can we apply effective differentiation practices to meet the needs of our students?"

The following is a brief summary of what current research reveals about mathematics instruction with gifted learners. We then recommend a model that teachers can use in mixed-ability classrooms to challenge students effectively and raise their achievement in mathematics.

Review of Research

Particularly in mathematics, research supports the academic effects of accelerated or advanced curricula for high-ability learners (VanTassel-Baska & Brown, 2005). Additionally, Kulik and Kulik's (1992) meta-analysis supported the notion that acceleration, when used in tandem with ability grouping, has stronger effects on student learning than enrichment. Similarly, Walberg (1991), in comparing acceleration to other strategies (e.g., independent study, various modes of grouping, and problem solving) found that acceleration showed powerful treatment effects and differentiated educational gains.

Research on the acceleration of mathematical strategies supports the use of increased pace and less repetition for advanced learners. In an investigation of a group of students in grades 7–12 identified as having high abilities in mathematics, Kolitch and Brody (1992) found that these students were successful when they took mathematics courses several years earlier than their same-age peers. In this study, students took calculus an average of 2.5 years before the pace suggested by traditional high school programs. In following these students, the researchers found that achievement in the accelerated calculus course and subsequent postcalculus courses was high. Students reported no difficulty or minimal difficulty in this type of acceleration, and most completed college math courses while still in high school.

Mills, Ablard, and Lynch (1992) investigated the effectiveness of shortened, accelerated mathematics courses with students identified as mathematically talented. Their study documented the use of individually paced summer courses by examining the students' success in their successive courses. The summer courses provided students the opportunity to complete entire courses in algebra, precalculus, and even calculus. After being accelerated during the summer program, students reported feeling well prepared for the courses following the summer course, and, in the majority of cases, the students maintained A averages.

Acceleration benefits are not specific to mathematical content. Lynch (1992) documented the effectiveness of "fast-paced" high school science courses for gifted students. The Center for Gifted Education at the College of William and Mary has conducted research that follows up on the effectiveness of accelerated pacing and advanced content for all subject areas (Van Tassel-Baska, Avery, Little, & Hughes, 2000; Van Tassel-Baska, Bass, Ries, Poland, & Avery, 1998; Van Tassel-Baska, Johnson, Hughes, & Boyce, 1996). This research helps to provide support for content acceleration and pacing of academic content.

Gifted Learners in the Mathematics Classroom

Gifted learners have cognitive differences that necessitate a differentiated approach to curricular and instructional practices within mathematics classrooms. One primary difference is gifted students' ability to acquire new and complex information more rapidly than their average-ability peers (Feldhusen, 1994; Sternberg, 1988).

Rogers (2000) revealed three vital insights into the cognitive difference of gifted learners in mathematics classrooms. First, the rate at which children with intelligence scores above 130 learn and process information is approximately eight times faster than children with intelligence scores below 70 (i.e., students identified as having serious mental deficiencies). Second, students with high abilities in mathematics are more likely to retain science and mathematics content with almost complete accuracy when taught two or three times faster than the average class pace. Third, students with high abilities in math are more likely to forget or mislearn science and mathematics content when they review it more than two or three times. Taking these points into consideration, students with high abilities in mathematics will learn mathematical concepts with fewer repetitions than their average-ability peers. This difference presents a distinct challenge to the math teacher. More specifically, how can the needs of *all* students be met in one classroom?

One answer to this challenge can be found in a mixed-ability classroom, where questions arise such as "How does one manage an instructional program where a small group of students needs one or two repetitions of a new concept while the majority of the class needs four or five repetitions?" In reality, it is difficult to accelerate a cluster of students while maintaining a typical pace that uses multiple repetitions for the rest of the class.

There are several approaches to accelerating and differentiating instructional and curricular strategies for advanced students, including telescoping the curriculum and tiered objectives.

Telescoping

Telescoping is curriculum compacting. It may involve compacting up to 3 years of the curriculum into 2 academic years or 2 years of the curriculum into 1 academic year. Telescoping is a logical approach to mathematics differentiation because of the linear nature of the skills in the curriculum, and telescoping has produced documented achievement gains for students at the secondary level (Lynch, 1992; Mills et al., 1992).

As promising as the benefits of telescoping appear, it still presents instructional difficulty in terms of managing a flexible pace in a mixed-ability classroom. However, a tiered-objectives model can provide a manageable and effective method for telescoping the mathematics curriculum in a mixed-ability setting (Tomlinson, 1999).

Tiered Objectives

Tiered objectives and tiered activities are ways for teachers to ensure that students work at appropriate levels of challenge while studying the same essential skills and concepts. The guidelines for developing tiered activities include four different parts (Tomlinson, 1999):

1. Identify the objectives, concepts, and skills to be taught.
2. Create a set of activities for teaching that objective for students working on grade level.
3. Identify the next level of increasing complexity. Then, develop a set of activities to teach the same concept at an increased level of complexity. This same step can be replicated for more than one tier if desired.
4. Group students according to assessed levels of readiness and assign them to the set of activities for the different tiers.

The practice of tiered mathematics objectives has two underlying assumptions. First, students with high abilities in mathematics will learn new concepts with fewer repetitions than their peers. Second, mathematics objectives are logically sequenced by grade level and concepts are replicated in successive years with increasing difficulty. Teachers sometimes think of telescoping as a linear process, rather than a layered process.

When envisioned as a linear process, teachers and program directors understand acceleration as occurring in a specific, preestablished progression. In other words, if asked to complete a two-in-one telescope of the curriculum, a sixth-grade teacher may imagine teaching all the sixth-grade objectives before Christmas and all the seventh-grade objectives between January and Memorial Day. If asked to complete a three-in-two telescope, she may imagine completing the sixth-grade curriculum and then completing the first half of the seventh-grade curriculum in the last 2 or 3 months of the academic year. However, this view is not congruent with what works best for teachers or students.

When the practice of tiered objectives is viewed as a layered telescoping model, rather than a linear telescoping model, the general curriculum map of the academic year is based upon completing one grade-level set of learner objectives (e.g., all sixth-grade objectives). The telescoping occurs during the repetitions of these objectives. Advanced students learn each concept or skill at 2 years' worth of complexity in the same number or repetitions a typical learner acquires the grade-level knowledge. As the typical learner will need four or five repetitions to master a concept, the gifted learner masters the grade-level objective in one or two. While the majority of the class is still working on the grade-level expectation of a given concept, the gifted learner is solving problems based on the increased complexity of a tiered objective of the concept (e.g., seventh-grade objective, rather than sixth). When this model is applied to all objectives in a content area, it is possible for a student to master the curriculum expectations of two grade levels in one year, even given the management complexities of a mixed-ability classroom.

An Example of Teaching Scaled Objectives

The following example uses sixth-grade mathematics as a starting point. Table 6.1 presents the parallel sequence (based on the Texas Essential Knowledge and Skills) of how the learner objectives increase in complexity from grades 6–8.

After introducing the concept of angle measurement and modeling how to measure angles, the teacher could have students work in small groups to measure angles related to objects around the room and label the angles with the appropriate classification according to their angle measures. After the small-group practice, individual students could be given a set of different triangles or quadrilaterals. As the rest of the class measures the angles and predicts a relationship, students with high abilities in mathematics may work independently to master the necessary concepts and terms, while other students benefit from repetitions with the original content. Students with high abilities in mathematics can be challenged and accelerated by applying angle measurement to concepts that would normally be taught in the seventh-grade curriculum, such as complementary and supplementary angles, as well as similar figures.

In gaining mastery of these higher grade-level objectives, students could use geometry exploration software or pencils and paper to set up a diagram of two adjacent angles that form a complementary (right) or a supplementary (straight) angle. Students may also manipulate the common ray in the interior of the right angle and straight angle to record the resulting measurement of each independent angle (see Figure 6.1). Equations of these measurement pairs could be displayed in a table. If students master this concept quickly, then the teacher can continue to accelerate them with eighth-grade concepts, such as exploring the relationship between corresponding angles in a variety of geometric figures.

Conclusion

Educators should provide *all* learners with opportunities to obtain optimal levels of learning. Many, if not most, classrooms include learners with mixed abilities. Particularly in mathematics classes, these learner differences may be significant. In order to attain optimal levels of learning for *all* students, instructional leaders must move beyond the one-size-fits-all conception of curricular and instructional practices. Rather, the

Table 6.1. **Scaling of Learning Objectives Examples of Scope and Sequence**

Grade 6 Mathematics (Geometry)	Grade 7 Mathematics (Geometry)	Grade 8 Mathematics (Geometry)
The student will demonstrate an understanding of numbers, operations, and qualitative reasoning.	The student will demonstrate an understanding of numbers, operations, and qualitative reasoning.	The student will demonstrate an understanding of numbers, operations, and qualitative reasoning.
(6.6) The student uses geometric vocabulary to describe angles, polygons, and circles. The student is expected to:	(7.6) The student compares and classifies shapes and solids using geometric vocabulary and properties. The student is expected to:	(8.6) The student uses transformational geometry to develop spatial sense. The student is expected to:
(a) use angle measurement to classify angles as acute, obtuse, or right; (b) identify relationships involving angles in triangles and quadrilaterals; and (c) describe the relationship between radius, diameter, and circumference of a circle.	(a) use angle measurements to classify pairs of angles as complementary or supplementary; (b) use properties to classify shapes including triangles, quadrilaterals, pentagons, and circles; (c) use properties to classify solids, including pyramids, cones, prisms, and cylinders; (d) use critical attributes to define similarity.	(a) generate similar shapes using dilations including enlargements and reductions; and (b) graph dilations, reflections, and translations on a coordinate plane.

Note. Objectives were taken from the Texas Essential Knowledge and Skills published in Chapter 111 of the Texas Education Code.

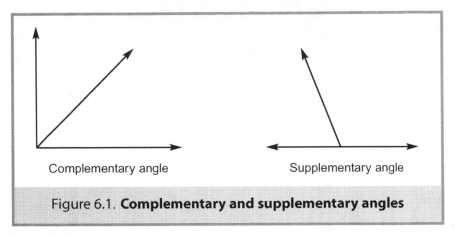

Complementary angle   Supplementary angle

Figure 6.1. **Complementary and supplementary angles**

curriculum should include a sequence of learning activities that is constantly being developed in response to learner readiness, which includes the point at which a student enters a particular study and the pace at which he or she acquires new knowledge and skills.

Differentiating curricular and instructional practices requires that teachers modify the depth and complexity of concepts, as well as the pace of instruction. Current best practice research indicates that acceleration strategies, such as working with above-grade-level objectives and completing multiple levels of curricula in a year, provides significant academic benefits. Applying tiered objectives accomplishes the principles and benefits of acceleration while maintaining a manageable framework for teachers.

Recommendations

Teachers or program coordinators interested in implementing tiered objectives as an accelerated program option need opportunities to work with content-based vertical teams to align curricular objectives. This can be accomplished by having all teachers in a subject or content area, regardless of grade level, identify where the objectives meet and overlap. Tiering objectives occurs when teachers can easily access and identify the objectives across grade levels that are sequenced with those they personally teach. It is recommended that teachers in vertical teams develop objective charts similar to the example in Table 6.1 so that objectives can be conceptualized as being fluid. Doing so will allow teachers to think about teaching concepts in a field of study, rather than teaching Chapter 7 in the textbook. If teachers are unable to explore objectives as interrelated, they may not quickly see how the concepts in Chapter 7 in the sixth-grade textbook correspond to the same concept taught at a higher level of complexity in Chapter 5 of the seventh-grade textbook. Allowing teachers to work in vertical teams encourages them to teach concepts, rather than chunks of knowledge and skills.

School curricular documents could include not only an aligned sequence of concepts and objectives, but also information about grade-level resources such as textbooks that are available to teach specific objectives. Creating a reference system in this manner provides teachers with resources (such as texts and materials) at a variety of grade levels. Having such resources available increases teachers' abilities to meet the needs of all students. Unfortunately, teachers often report that their campus administrators or department chairs will not allow them to use textbooks from other grade levels. Access to a variety of resources allows every student to have an opportunity to achieve his or her optimal level of learning. Thus, teachers must have access to the resources that will assist student learning.

The tiered objectives model is guided by the principle that teachers can teach one concept to the whole class, while students develop knowledge and skills related to that concept at different levels of complexity. The essence of this strategy is undermined if teachers are not equipped with proper resources to teach concepts at each student's point of entry.

References

Feldhusen, J. F. (1994). Learning and cognition in talented youth. In J. VanTassel-Baska (Ed.), *Comprehensive curriculum for gifted learners* (2nd ed., pp. 17–28). Boston: Allyn and Bacon.

Kolitch, E. R., & Brody, L. E. (1992). Mathematics acceleration of highly talented students: An evaluation. *Gifted Child Quarterly, 36*, 78–86.

Kulik, J. A., & Kulik, C. C. (1992). Meta-analytic findings on grouping programs. *Gifted Child Quarterly, 36,* 73–77.

Lynch, S. J. (1992). Fast-paced high school science for academically talented: A 6-year perspective. *Gifted Child Quarterly, 36,* 147–154.

Mills, C. J., Ablard, K. E., & Lynch, S. J. (1992). Academically talented students' preparation for advanced-level coursework after individually-paced precalculus class. *Journal for the Education of the Gifted, 16,* 2–17.

Rogers, K. B. (2000, December). *Lessons learned in the 20th century to help us in the 21st.* Paper presented at the annual meeting of the Texas Association for the Gifted and Talented, Austin.

Sternberg, R. J. (1988). Intelligence. In R. J. Sternberg & E. E. Smith (Eds.), *The psychology of human thought* (pp. 267–308). New York: Cambridge University Press.

Tomlinson, C. A. (1999). *The differentiated classroom: Responding to the needs of all learners.* Alexandria, VA: Association for Supervision and Curriculum Development.

VanTassel-Baska, J., Avery, L. D., Little, C. A., & Hughes, C. E. (2000). An evaluation of the implementation: The impact of the William and Mary units on schools. *Journal for the Education of the Gifted, 23,* 244–272.

VanTassel-Baska, J., Bass, G., Ries, R., Poland, D., & Avery, L. D. (1998). A national study of science curriculum effectiveness with high-ability students. *Gifted Child Quarterly, 42,* 200–211.

VanTassel-Baska, J., & Brown, E. F. (2005). An analysis of gifted education curriculum models. In F. A. Karnes & S. M. Bean (Eds.), *Methods and materials for teaching the gifted* (2nd ed., pp. 75–106). Waco, TX: Prufrock Press.

VanTassel-Baska, J., Johnson, D. T., Hughes, C. E., & Boyce, L. N. (1996). A study of language arts curriculum effectiveness with gifted learners. *Journal for the Education of the Gifted, 19,* 461–480.

Walberg, H. (1991). Productive teaching and instruction: Assessing the knowledge base. In H. C. Waxman & H. J. Walberg (Eds.), *Effective teaching: Current research* (pp. 33–62). Berkeley, CA: McCutchan.

chapter 7

Breaking Down the Barriers
adventures in teaching single-sex algebra classes

by **Susan Lee Stutler**

On the first day of middle school, the teacher introduced herself to her class of 18 excited math students newly arrived in the Advanced Placement Algebra class. These students had come to her from participating in a gifted elementary math program they had substituted for regular math. They had also obtained the necessary qualifying score on a district math skills placement test.

After a brief introduction and a course overview, the teacher asked the students to look around their new environment and see if they could find anything missing or if they noticed anything unusual about the class. The students did so, but upon finding nothing out of the ordinary, they waited expectantly for class to begin. At the end of the 50-minute period, the teacher again asked the pupils if they had noticed anything missing. They hadn't, and class was dismissed.

Hours later, another group of 18 mathematically adept students filed into the classroom, having qualified for the AP Algebra course via the same gifted elementary math program and having obtained the same qualifying scores on the district measure. Before the teacher could finish introducing herself, however, these students did notice something different about the class, and the question spilled forth: "Where are the boys?" The previous class, which had been all boys, hadn't noticed the absence of female students, but the second class, which was all girls, immediately noted the absence of male students.

So began the odyssey of this middle school math teacher's yearlong adventure in teaching single-sex algebra courses. What began as an expedient and somewhat whimsical method of reducing class size became a unique opportunity to observe differences in the learning styles of mathematically gifted boys and girls. The resulting success of the 18 adolescent girls serves to support gifted girls' needs for a learning environment that minimizes obstacles to female achievement such as the fear of success phenomenon and societal messages concerning conformity and femininity. Advocates of the need to help gifted girls often encourage the idea of single-sex learning environments for some students and mentors for gifted girls (Kerr, 1994).

For many years, we teachers at the elementary level watched in dismay as our extremely bright, confident, enthusiastic young female mathematicians qualified into advanced middle school math courses where the majority of them suddenly and unaccountably lost confidence in themselves, faltered, and eventually withdrew from advanced courses completely. Only an extremely small proportion of the girls forged ahead into the realms of geometry and trigonometry.

These profoundly gifted, determined nonconformists have been described by Barbara Kerr in her book *Smart Girls Two: A New Psychology of Girls, Women, and Giftedness* (1994) as being "so bright and motivated that their intellect simply will not focus on social expectations" (p. 125). However, the majority of the girls failed to succeed even though they were certainly capable of success. These girls had been placed into elementary math programs based upon scores at the 97th percentile or higher on the quantitative portion of the Cognitive Abilities Test (CogAT) and had scored at the 90th percentile or higher on the district skills test. These girls had demonstrated not only mathematical knowledge, but they had scored in the top 3% in the nation in mathematical reasoning ability.

In the 2 years preceding the advent of the single-sex algebra class, the success rate for the girls was less than 10%, mostly because of poor grades and failure. Given that these gifted girls were in the top 3% districtwide, only 0.3% percent of the total female population successfully navigated the advanced coursework. On the other hand, the success rate for the boys was nearly 80%.

What might account for these girls' frustrating lack of success once they reached middle school? Could it be that they were not developmentally ready for the abstract operational thinking so necessary to algebra, as some in the district suggested? Was this failure a clear indication of the old notion that boys were simply more inclined toward mathematical understandings? Or were there other, more complicated factors at work? At the elementary level, we shook our heads helplessly, determined to work harder at fortifying our young charges with motivation, confidence, and skill, all seemingly to no avail.

It was certainly intriguing when startling stories began trickling down to elementary teachers about heroic female math conquests in the new single-sex algebra class. Former students reported that the two math classes had taken their first exam and that the girls had done very well—even scoring significantly higher than the boys. Indeed, this auspicious start marked the beginning of a year of superior female achievement. Upon meeting this outstanding middle school teacher and discovering that she kept an educational journal of her observations, I asked if I might use her data along with other measures to uncover what factors in this single-sex environment might contribute to the girls' success. Comparing year-end grades and placement results, district test scores, teacher and student interviews, a student survey, along with the teacher's observations, I hoped to describe more elaborately the dramatic success achieved in 1 year by 18 dauntless girls. I began my study with a review of the literature concerning gifted girls.

The World of Gifted Adolescent Girls

In considering the achievement rates of adolescent girls, researchers have accumulated evidence that points to many barriers to female success and the well-documented "adolescent plunge." Loeb and Jay (1987), reporting on the self-concept of gifted girls, indicate that girls in grades 4–6 find giftedness an advantage, possess a positive self-image, and demonstrate a more internal locus of control than nongifted females. Adolescence, however, a time of growth, change, and challenging situations for all students, may be a particularly distressing period in the life of gifted girls. In addition to the difficult choices rampant during adolescence, gifted girls may be faced with the real or perceived choices of popularity versus high achievement; conformity and group acceptance versus the relative isolation of academic acceleration; and societal expectations of femininity versus involvement in stereotypically male arenas such as higher level math courses. Between the ages of 11 and 15, peer relationships become prominent in girls' lives, and a shift from achievement to social acceptance and love needs begins (Groth, 1969). Sadker and Sadker (1982) found that, while male and female achievement scores are nearly equal at the age of 9, by the age of 13 there is a decline in the achievement of girls. While girls are outspoken and confident as children, by age 11 they lose confidence in themselves, their looks, and their abilities (Rogers & Gilligan, 1988). This research parallels Kline and Short's (1991) findings of a progressive decline in girls' self-perceived abilities and confidence and in their perception that others value their abilities. A decline in the achievement of gifted adolescent girls is evident in academic achievement test scores, course choices, and other academic goals (Kerr, 1997).

The often mixed and sometimes ambivalent messages society sends young gifted girls may present a serious barrier to their success in academic endeavors. The feminine grails for most adolescent girls are physical beauty, popularity, and conformity (Bell, 1989; Kerr, 1994; Taylor, Gilligan, & Sullivan, 1995). Compliant, nonaggressive behaviors are fostered and encouraged in girls through commercials, television, movies, fairy tales, and literature and are rewarded by parents, teachers, and friends (Reis & Dobyns, 1991). In middle school, when the issue of popularity becomes one of deep concern to most girls and when behavior out of the norm may be cause for ostracism, gifted girls often begin to hide or deny their giftedness and downplay their accomplishments (Kline & Short, 1991; Noble, 1989).

Other obstacles to adolescent female achievement include fear of success and the tendency to attribute success to luck or effort, rather than ability. The Homer Effect (Homer, 1972), also known as the Fear of Success Syndrome, has been repeatedly shown to affect girls' performance when in competition against boys. The girl will unconsciously and consistently lower her own ability so that the boy may win. Research suggests that the perceived task value decreases when weighed against the consequences of achievement (Parsons et al., 1983). The desire to win decreases when compared with the effect of winning—the perceived loss of femininity. Among highly gifted female adolescents, the motive to avoid success is highly prevalent (Hollinger & Fleming, 1984; Lavach & Lanier, 1975). Girls in competition will compromise in order to preserve intimacy (Tannen, 1990). However, this hypothesis does not take into account that girls are more likely to perform below their ability level when in competition with boys than with other girls (Kerr, 1994).

The Impostor Phenomenon (Clance & Imes, 1978), another common barrier to female success, occurs when a gifted female believes that she has been, in effect, fooling those around her concerning her perceived high abilities. She denies her intelligence, writes off her achievements, and attributes any success to factors such as chance, luck, or other external forces. Noble (1989) found it remarkable that so few women "realize they are gifted despite years of evidence to the contrary" (p.133). On the other hand, bright young males more often attribute academic and other successful experiences to ability, effort, or both (Deaux & Emswiller, 1974). As a result, when gifted adolescent girls are confronted with the intense demands of higher level math courses, they may convince themselves that somehow there's been a mistake; that everybody else in the class is actually smarter than they; and that, since you can't fool all of the people all of the time, it may be time to get out.

Hollinger and Fleming (1984) found that these and other internal barriers, such as nonassertiveness, were major issues in the achievement of gifted and talented girls and that the barriers were interrelated and correlated with personality attributes such as expressiveness and instrumentality, both of which are central to achievement (Hollinger & Fleming). *Expressiveness* is the self-perception of being adept at interpersonal relationships; expressive girls are empathetic, caring, and communicative. While these girls are highly sensitive to the needs of others, they also display a high degree of self-awareness. *Instrumentality* may be described as one's sense of agency; the perception that one's actions and opinions have an impact on the environment. High-achieving girls make decisions and take risks, firm in the belief that the decisions they make and the risks they take will make a difference. Kerr (1997) has suggested that gifted girls need to be encouraged to take risks throughout their educational experience because it is important that they know that their decisions have weight. Kerr also suggested that "teachers may need to reverse the common practice of rewarding compliant behavior and withdrawing rewards for, or even punishing, noisy and nonconforming behavior" (p. 493).

The All-Girls Learning Environment

In the middle school single-sex algebra class, opportunities for expressiveness and instrumentality were ripe, and the stage was set for 18 girls to break through the barriers. The teacher described the girls in the class as being "thinkers without conflict." By this she meant that, although the act of thinking itself requires conflict, that conflict should emanate from the learning to be done or the problem to be solved and not from extraneous events in the environment.

The opening scene in this chapter is remarkably illustrative of one difference in attitude and perception between gifted adolescent boys and gifted adolescent girls. The boys hadn't even noticed that the girls were missing. They had been ready for algebra; that's what they were there for, and they wanted to get to it. There were simply no other considerations. The girls, on the other hand, immediately noticed the boys' absence. The first words out of their mouths were, "Where are the boys?" As the research demonstrates, girls in middle school become highly concerned with issues of popularity, which include conforming to the feminine ideal and being perceived as feminine by boys. The removal of the boys from the learning environment in many ways freed the girls for productive thinking experiences.

Almost immediately, the teacher noticed slight changes in the girls' attitudes and demeanor. As the weeks went by, the girls began to relax; they took their shoes off, untucked their shirts, clipped their hair up, leaned back in their chairs or got comfortable on the floor. If at any time a girl had to leave the classroom, however, the shirt was tucked back in, the hair came down, was brushed, and mirrors were checked. When someone didn't feel well, a quiet and comfortable resting place was created for her. The girls liked to celebrate achievement with parties, food, and drink to which they all contributed. At such times, they always remembered the boys' class, as well, and provided them with cupcakes and cookies. The teacher pointed out that it was the girls themselves who created this nurturing environment, without her direction. She did however, permit it, and thus the girls were able to explore their needs for expressiveness. The boys would also occasionally plan a celebration, and then, almost invariably, they would forget to bring the necessary accouterments.

Questioning Styles

The teacher noted two distinctive questioning styles that emerged in her classes.

The boys asked few questions as new material was introduced, and those questions that were asked usually concerned directions. Typically, the boys got straight to work and asked more in-depth questions only if they hit a snag, at which time they required individual attention. Once they received help, they again worked steadily until the next snag.

The girls, however, would sometimes ask questions for as long as 20 minutes before beginning their work. These questions could entail almost every aspect of what they might encounter as they solved algebraic problems. Many of the questions involved "what if" suppositions that then led to theoretical discussions. According to the teacher, the girls in her previous coed classes had not usually asked these types of questions. In the single-sex environment, the girls found themselves able to question, as well as posit ideas, without the real or perceived fear of ridicule or loss of femininity. The girls took turns teaching and helping each other with their algebra. No one girl led the group; at various times, each emerged as a leader. These leadership roles also occurred in the boys' class. The teacher recalled however, that only rarely in her previous coed classes had girls emerged as leaders.

Competition

As the girls' faith in their own instrumentality grew, it became apparent that they were not only unafraid of competition, but they enjoyed competing with each other and relished the opportunity to compete with the boys' class. It was interesting to note that the Homer Effect was simply not in evidence in the single-sex math class. Thus, the excitement and enthusiasm with which the girls threw themselves into besting the boys on quizzes and tests may be viewed against the enumerable and well-documented, occasions when girls lose in order to please or in an attempt to conform to societal standards of femininity. Indeed, the teacher admitted that, at first, she was somewhat shocked at the high degree of competitive spirit being demonstrated by the girls. Her immediate inclination was to discourage their zeal, but some instinct cautioned her against it. She did not explicitly reward this noisy, nonconforming, unladylike behavior, but, once again, she allowed it.

Problem Solving and Hands-On Projects

The teacher, as in years past, provided both classrooms with numerous opportunities for problem solving and hands-on math projects. The students explored algebraic concepts with metric blocks and other manipulatives. The teacher made use of community resources and recruited businesspeople to speak to her classes. The classes experimented with weight and stress loads, and an architect helped the students develop bridge-building plans, which were then implemented.

Much more often than in her previous experiences, the teacher began to answer questions about opportunities for women in the fields of math and science. She often stressed the importance of the advanced math and science coursework that would enable these students to enroll in the college programs of their choice. The teacher, well into uncharted territory, had discovered herself in the roles of guide and mentor, as well as teacher, to 18 young explorers.

Achievement

The single-sex algebra class afforded the girls with opportunities to think and solve problems in an environment less permeated with societal expectations of femininity that also allowed for expressiveness and instrumentality. Almost by accident, they were also receiving the experience and guidance of a mentor.

What effect, if any, would these experiences have on their achievement? A look at the end-of-year grades and the next year's placement results for the 18 girls showed a significant improvement. Fourteen of the girls earned A's; an overall score of 90% or higher, and the remaining four girls earned B's, a score of 80% or above. Additionally, all of the girls went on to participate in a high school geometry course the next year. Of the boys, only one earned an A. There were 11 B's, 4 C's (an overall score of 70%), and 2 D's (a score of 60% or above). Sixteen of the boys went on to participate in the high school geometry class the next year. Thus, it is interesting to note that, although the boys' performance was comparable to previous years, the girls' increase in performance was almost staggering.

Attitudes About the Single-Sex Math Class

Perhaps even more intriguing is the comparison of the boys' and girls' responses to an attitude survey conducted during the closing weeks of the school year. Students were asked to provide a response of "no difference," "coed," or "same sex" to each of eight questions. Space for comments was provided.

When asked, "In which type of class are you more likely to ask questions?," all but two of the girls responded "same sex," and much of the accompanying commentary concerned the fact that they felt less fear of ridicule in the same-sex environment. The boys' responses to the same question indicated that there was "no difference." The same results were obtained for questions such as "In which type of class are you most likely to participate?" and "In which type of class are you most comfortable?" In fact, while the boys consistently indicated that the sex of their classmates made no difference to their academic performance, the girls indicated that not only did they achieve a higher grade average in same-sex math classes, but they believed that their overall understanding of math concepts was greater in the same-sex setting, as well.

Conclusion

Mathematically gifted girls drop out of advanced and accelerated math courses at an alarming rate and choose the kind of watered-down coursework that precludes them from continuing their education in the fields of math or science (Kerr, 1994; Sells, 1980). It is imperative that we as educators find a way to turn this tide. Is it possible to draw conclusions and make recommendations for the education of gifted female adolescents based upon results gleaned from this almost accidental voyage of discovery? In discussing gender differences in achievement and variables that can be manipulated, Callahan (1979) urged that we recognize the fact that "underlying the problems of achievement and motivation of gifted and talented females lie hypotheses yet to be tested and perhaps untestable in the experimental tradition" (p. 412).

The often intense educational and philosophical debate between those who expound the egalitarian tenets of inclusive educational settings for all students and those who advocate differentiated curricula and educational settings for the gifted continues to swirl. In this atmosphere, advocacy of single-sex educational opportunities may be viewed by some as an attempt at further separation. Certainly, there is a need for more research to determine the effects of single-sex educational experiences upon both male and female achievement. However, the conspicuous academic gains achieved by the 18 females in this middle school single-sex math class are, at the very least, an indication that the needs of mathematically gifted adolescent girls may be better served in an nonthreatening environment that provides opportunities for expressiveness and instrumentality, as well as permission to deviate from the societal expectations of feminine behavior. Female role-models and mentors can help gifted girls develop an attitude of thinking for success, rather than fear of success. If single-sex educational experiences offer gifted adolescent females a chance to become "thinkers without conflict," then we should give them that chance.

References

Bell, L. A. (1989). Something's wrong here and it's not me: Challenging the dilemmas that block girls' success. *Journal for the Education of the Gifted, 12,* 118–129.

Callahan, C. M. (1979). The gifted and talented woman. In A. H. Passow (Ed.), *The gifted and talented* (pp. 401–423). Chicago: National Society for the Study of Education.

Clance, P. R., & Imes, S. A. (1978). The impostor phenomenon in high achieving women: Dynamics end therapeutic intervention. *Psychotherapy: Theory, Research and Practice, 15,* 241–245.

Deaux, K., & Emswiller, T. (1974). Explanations of successful performance in sex linked tasks: What's skill for the male is luck for the female. *Journal of Personality and Social Psychology, 29,* 80–85.

Groth, N. J. (1969). *Vocational development for gifted girls.* (ERIC Document Reproduction Service No. ED931747)

Hollinger, C. L., & Fleming, E. S. (1984). Internal barriers to the realization of potential: Correlates and interrelationships among gifted and talented female adolescents. *Gifted Child Quarterly, 28,* 135–139.

Homer, M. S. (1972). Toward an understanding of achievement-related conflicts in women. *Journal of Social Issues, 28,* 157–175.

Kerr, B. A. (1994). *Smart girls two: A new psychology of girls, women, and giftedness.* Dayton: Ohio Psychology Press.

Kerr, B. A. (1997). Developing talents in girls and young women. In N. Colangelo & G. A. Davis (Eds.), *Handbook of gifted education* (pp. 483–497). Boston: Allyn and Bacon.

Kline, B. E., & Short, E. B. (1991). Changes in emotional resilience: Gifted adolescent females. *Roeper Review, 13,* 118–121.

Lavach, J. F., & Lanier, H. B. (1975). The motive to avoid success in 7th, 8th, 9th, and 10th grade high-achieving girls. *Journal of Educational Research, 68,* 216–218.

Loeb, R. C., & Jay, G. (1987). Self-concept in gifted children: Differential impact in boys and girls. *Gifted Child Quarterly, 31,* 9–13.

Noble, K. D. (1989). Counseling gifted women: Becoming the heroes of our own stories. *Journal for the Education of the Gifted, 12,* 131–141.

Parsons, J. E., Adler, T. F., Futterman, R., Goff, S. B., Kaczala, C. M., Meece, J. L., & Midgley, C. (1983). General model of academic choice. In J. T. Spence (Ed.), *Perspectives on achievement and achievement motivation*. San Francisco: Freeman.

Reis, S. M., & Dobyns, S. M. (1991). An annotated bibliography of non-fictional books and curricular materials to encourage gifted females. *Roeper Review, 13*, 129–134.

Rogers, A., & Gilligan, C. (1988). *Translating girls voices: Two languages of development.* Cambridge, MA: Harvard University Graduate School of Education Project on the Psychology of Women and the Development of Girls.

Sadker, M., & Sadker, D. (1982). *Sex equity handbook for schools.* New York: Longman.

Sells, L. W. (1980). The mathematics filter and the education of women and minorities. In L. H. Fox, L. Brody, & D. Tobin (Eds.), *Women and the mathematical mystique* (pp. 66–75). Baltimore, MD: Johns Hopkins University Press.

Tannen, D. (1990). *You just don't understand: Women and men in conversation.* New York: Ballantine Books.

Taylor, J. M., Gilligan, C., & Sullivan, A. M. (1995). *Between voice and silence.* Cambridge, MA: Harvard University Press.

chapter 8

Math in Architecture

*using technology to connect
math to the real world*

by **Mary Christopher**

*I*magine two classrooms. One contains children involved in fun activities that spark interest and encourage high levels of thinking, but have little connection to what is occurring in the regular curriculum. Students approach the activities with enthusiasm and excitement and leave the classroom with pleasant memories and new perspectives.

Another classroom contains students involved in studying content in-depth or at advanced levels while making connections to the real world and using technology to enhance the process. The children are challenged to approach the core content just as experts in that discipline would. They leave the learning experience with new knowledge and refined skills.

While both classrooms have characteristics that may benefit gifted children, the second one prepares the students to function in future careers. By applying the knowledge gained in the school setting to new situations, the students will be able to carry this learning with them throughout their lives.

Math and Technology Standards

How might teachers of gifted children begin to change their programs to meet the challenges of the future? Looking at local and national standards developed as a result of reform initiatives in mathematics and technology may serve as a starting point and as a support system for helping teachers make changes. Gifted educators can use these standards to plan curricula centered on knowledge and skills that will move students into the new century.

Three recent documents have influenced gifted education by shifting the focus of programs in gifted education toward standards within specific content areas. In 1989, the Commission on Standards for School Mathematics (CSSM) of the National Council of Teachers of Mathematics (NCTM) published *Curriculum and Evaluation Standards for School Mathematics* in response to the call for reform and the establishment of national standards. Additionally, the *Report to the President on the Use of Technology to Strengthen K–12 Education in the United States* (Panel on Educational Technology, 1997) described the current status of technology in public schools and emphasized the need for a change in how technology is used in America's schools. In my state, the *Texas State Plan for the Education of Gifted/Talented Students* (Division of Advanced Academic Services, 1996) identified three levels of accountability in gifted education and requires the implementation of a comprehensive program for grades 1–12.

Impact of Reform Initiatives

The 1996 Texas publication created in many gifted and talented programs in Texas a shift from an enrichment model to a content-based one. This shift occurred because one of the compliance standards states that learning experiences for gifted and talented students should "emphasize content from the four core academic areas" (Division of Advanced Academic Services, 1996; see 19 TAC 89.3). The gifted curriculum must be based on science, social studies, math, and language arts; must challenge gifted learners; and must be differentiated to meet their needs.

Given new standards, the teacher might consider restructuring the curriculum for the gifted learner in mathematics. Although the Curriculum and Evaluation Standards for School Mathematics (CSSM, 1989) were not developed specifically for gifted education, they can be used as a philosophical support to the gifted program. The National Council for Teachers of Mathematics developed the following five tenets for their standards:

- learning to value mathematics;
- becoming confident in one's ability;
- becoming a mathematical problem solver;
- learning to communicate mathematically; and
- learning to reason mathematically (CSSM, pp. 5–6).

While these principles support mathematics education for all students, they also serve as goals for educating gifted learners in this content area. New mathematical knowledge emerges from problem solving that uses the students' individual abilities and allows them to reason and communicate mathematically. Through this problem-solving process, students develop an understanding of the depth and complexity of mathematical concepts.

Another area to consider when planning curricula for gifted learners is the use of technology within the curriculum. In their report, the Panel on Education Technology (1997) made these two recommendations:

- focus on learning *with* technology, not *about* technology; and
- emphasize content and pedagogy, and not just hardware (p. 7).

Children experience growth in technological knowledge and skills as they use these skills in authentic situations. Technology should be embedded in the curriculum, rather than taught as a separate subject. This recommendation is particularly true for gifted learners because they acquire new knowledge at a rapid pace and can apply that knowledge at high levels. Gifted students should be given opportunities to use technology to solve real-world problems and to produce top-quality products within the core content areas.

By combining the standards of the three reform initiatives discussed in this chapter, educators can plan for authentic learning experiences in mathematics for gifted learners. These students frequently approach a learning task with a vast amount of prior knowledge and are able to acquire new knowledge and construct their own meaning while completing the task. Once the task is completed, the meaning gained becomes part of the students' own knowledge base, allowing them to apply integrated concepts to new situations in the future.

Connecting Math to the Real World

For gifted learners to use mathematics and technology in authentic ways, teachers must plan problem-solving activities with real-world applications. The problem solving activity described in this article connects geometry and architecture using the drawing tools of an integrated software package. This performance task has been used successfully with fourth- and fifth-grade gifted children, but could be used effectively with middle school and high school students, as well. It could also be used as a model to develop other problem-solving activities for gifted learners.

The NCTM standards support the teaching of a broad range of topics, including probability, statistics, and geometry, but they also state that "they should be taught as an integrated whole, not as isolated topics" (CSSM, 1989, p. 87). These topics are not often covered in the regular mathematics curriculum because they are usually included in the last sections of textbooks that are often skipped by many teachers because of a lack of time.

An excellent way of solving the problem of limited time is by connecting these topics to other content areas and to real-world situations. The performance task, "Math in Architecture" (see Figure 8.1), provides a way for students to see geometric shapes and patterns in the facades of buildings while relying on prior knowledge or research about architectural terms and periods. After the students develop an understanding of geometric and architectural concepts, they compare two buildings, one res-

Problem:
Using the drawing feature of an integrated software package, students will replicate the facade of two buildings—one urban and one residential. They will analyze the geometric features and patterns found in the architectural structure of each building. Furthermore, they will compare the two types of buildings, referring to the architectural features.

Age Group:
Grades 2–5

Content Connection:
Math, Technology Applications, Science, Social Studies, Art, and Language Arts

Essential Questions:
*   What types of geometric patterns and shapes are used in the architecture of urban or residential buildings?
*   How are these two types of structures similar or different?

Materials:
*   Building materials: wooden blocks, Duplos, LEGOS, Lincoln Logs
*   Integrated computer software package: Microsoft Office
*   Computer assisted design software and/or hardware (optional)
*   Camera (digital camera preferred but not necessary)
*   Printer

Background Material:
Much of this information would be part of the regular curriculum of some grade levels. However, students can also research information in these areas for solving this problem:

*   Geometric shapes (e.g., squares, triangles, circles, semi-circles, cube, rectangular prisms)
*   Geometric patterns (e.g., single, repeating, random)
*   Symmetry/asymmetry
*   Architectural features (e.g., type of roofs, style of windows, porches, porticoes, number of stories)
*   Periods of architecture (e.g., Colonial, Federal, Victorian)
*   Use of computer drawing program

continued on next page

Figure 8.1. **Problem-solving performance task: Math in architecture**

Criteria:

This is an open-ended assignment with criteria dependent on the age-level and readiness of the student. The teacher will need to adjust the criteria to meet these expectations.

1. The completed drawings should be clear replicas of your buildings.
2. The analysis and comparison of the two types of buildings should show a clear understanding of geometric shapes, patterns, symmetry, architectural features, and periods of architecture.
3. The product of this project should include the original pictures and computer-drawn replicas of an urban and a residential building along with a written analysis/comparison of the two buildings. The choice of product is student-selected.

Procedure:

1. Place transparencies of the facades of various buildings and/or houses on the overhead projector. Let students identify geometric shapes and patterns found in the buildings by drawing those shapes on the transparencies. Discuss the use of geometric features in the design of building.
2. Review the periods of architecture and use this knowledge to identify characteristics of the buildings on the transparencies that fit certain periods.
3. Identify symmetry and asymmetry in the buildings on the transparencies. Discuss why architects use symmetry/asymmetry in buildings to make them aesthetically pleasing or unique. You may want to discuss the connection of architecture and art.
4. Tour a downtown area taking pictures of buildings using a digital camera. Upon returning to school, download these pictures into the computer and print them out. If a digital camera is not available, use a regular camera and develop the pictures for the next day.
5. Ask students to bring pictures of residences, either their own home or ones from magazines.
6. Allow students to use building materials to make a rough replica of their buildings. More advanced students may not need this concrete approach, but it will help many students construct a geometric understanding of the structures.
7. Model for the students how to use the drawing mode of an integrated software package to replicate the facade of a building. Special attention should be paid to the geometric shapes and patterns found in the building because this will allow for ease of drawing the facade. For examples, the main part of the house is the shape of a square, so students will use the drawing tool to draw this section. Emphasize the use of duplication in a drawing program to allow for easier repetition of patterns.
8. Place students in pairs. One person in each pair should replicate a

downtown building while the other should replicate a residential building. Allow students to work on this project for two to three weeks,
depending upon your access to computers.

9. After the replicas are completed, encourage the student pairs to discuss similarities and differences in their two buildings. This discussion
should culminate in a written analysis/comparison of the two buildings.

10. Students should select a format for their completed product. Possible
products might be a brochure, a computer presentation, an oral presentation with overheads, a book, or a poster. Allow class time for students to share their products.

11. Evaluate students' work by using the evaluation form that is more effective for the needs and abilities of your class. The Team Evaluation form
was developed to evaluate the work of lower elementary students, while
the rubric may be more appropriate for upper elementary students' work.

Oote. Adapted from *Engaging Creative Thinking: Activities to Integrate Problem Solving,* by B. Kingore, 1998,
Abilene, TX: Professional Associates Publishing. Copyright ©1998 by Professional Associates Publishing.

idential and one urban, and write an analysis. This written
analysis encourages them to communicate while strengthening
their mathematical literacy.

The integrated use of technology in the same performance
task also motivates students to develop their computer skills along
with their math skills. Students practice computer skills while
developing an understanding of geometric concepts and patterns
found in real structures, and they create a product to display their
new understanding. Using an integrated software package and a
digital camera, students practice skills such as the use of a mouse,
the use of drawing tools, cutting and pasting items in a document,
word processing, the use of a digital camera, and planning a layout for a brochure or poster. As an added benefit, students
develop their visual and spatial perception as they replicate the
facade of the building from a picture into a computer drawn
image (see Figure 8.2). Individuals who are visually and spatially
gifted have few opportunities to develop these skills in the school
setting, so this task is particularly suited to them.

Example of Use in the Classroom

While teaching in a self-contained fifth-grade classroom for

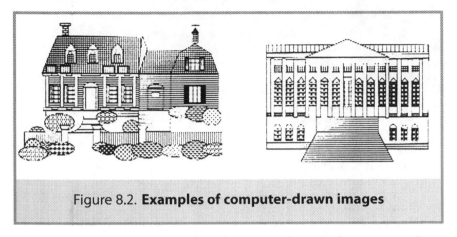

Figure 8.2. **Examples of computer-drawn images**

gifted students, I developed a unit of study that connected architecture to the content areas of history, mathematics, and science (Christopher, 1998). The unit included a historical study of periods of architecture; a look at the relationship of different types of houses to their surrounding habitats; problem-solving activities that involved the construction of bridges and towers; scale drawings of floor plans; the study of mathematical concepts related to architecture; and the "Math in Architecture" performance task included in this chapter.

The initial idea of this unit was inspired by the beautiful architecture found in downtown Louisville, Kentucky, which spans the late 1800s to the present time. Many of the buildings in Louisville have won architectural awards and are wonderful examples of different styles and periods of architecture. Because my elementary school was near the downtown area, we took a walking tour led by a professor from a local university, who identified and described the features of the buildings. He classified the buildings in the appropriate architectural period based on these features.

Using a digital camera, the students took pictures of the buildings's facades we saw on the walking tour. These pictures were downloaded onto our classroom computer when we returned to school. The students were able to access and print these pictures when they began working on the problem-solving performance task.

The culminating event of our study of architecture was the "Math in Architecture" activity. Students formed self-selected pairs to work on this activity in the computer lab. After a few instructions and a small amount of practice using computer tools to draw squares, circles, lines, and other geometric shapes, students began working on creating a replica of one of the downtown buildings and of a residential building of their choice. They were soon able to identify repeating patterns that helped to make the drawing more uniform and accelerated the drawing process.

When both drawings were completed, the students worked together to write a comparison of the two buildings. They used the comparison to create a product of their own choice. Many of the students created a brochure or poster, but some of them developed a computer slideshow to highlight their conclusions:

- Urban buildings tend to be more symmetrical than residential buildings.
- Contemporary buildings tend to be more asymmetrical.
- The entrance to urban buildings is usually large to allow more people to enter the building and to draw attention.
- Residential buildings are surrounded by landscape material that serves to soften the corners of the buildings.
- Urban buildings generally have multiple floors.
- Residential buildings are more horizontal than vertical in mass.
- The facade of both types of buildings is mainly created using rectangles, squares, and lines that have repeating patterns.
- A few circles and curves may be found in both types of buildings.

Students conducted a self-evaluation of their performance task using the "Team Evaluation" form (see Figure 8.3). This evaluation gave them the opportunity to identify their areas of strength and skill, as well as their potential growth areas in conceptual understanding, technology skills, and collaboration.

I evaluated the process and product of each student team using the Architecture Rubric (see Figure 8.4), which allowed me to give an objective analysis of the students' work. I found that most of the students were proficient in the use of technol-

Names: _____

Date: _____

Product: 35%

_____ Drawings are clear and precise.
_____ Evidence of geometric patterns and shapes is present.
_____ Product includes original picture and computer-drawn replicas.
_____ Layout of product is aesthetically pleasing.
_____ Selection of product enhances presentation of material.

Use of Technology: 20%

_____ Both members of team were able to use the drawing tools effectively.
_____ Product was saved and printed properly.
_____ Word processing technique enhances the product.

Comparison/Analysis: 35%

_____ Analysis of each building shows an understanding of geometric shapes, patterns, and symmetry.
_____ Comparison of two buildings shows clear understanding of math concepts.
_____ Knowledge of architectural features is evident in final product.

Self-evaluation: 10%

We worked together well because

_____ .

My contributions to the team were

_____ .

My partner's contributions to the team were

_____ .

In the future, we would like

_____ .

Figure 8.3. **Team evaluation**

Note. Adapted from *Engaging Creative Thinking: Activities to Integrate Problem Solving,* by B. Kingore, 1998, Abilene, TX: Professional Associates Publishing. Copyright ©1998 by Professional Associates Publishing.

Names: _____

Date: _____

Points

Criteria	_____ 1 _____	_____ 2 _____	_____ 3 _____	_____ 4 _____
Use of Technology	Weak skills; use of technology detracts from process and product	Emerging skills; use of technology does not enhance process or product	Proficient in use of technology; uses technology as a tool to communicate	Use of technology enhances process and product; uses technology as a tool to communicate
Carried Out Plan	Did not complete plan or lacked plan	Completed with ongoing assistance	Completed plan; limited prompting needed	Followed through well; no prompting; exceeded expectations
Mathematical Content	Needs clarity and focus of mathematical ideas	Attempts to construct meaning connecting geometry and architecture	Analysis and comparison is clear and understandable; mathematical reasoning is evident	In-depth analysis and comparison; Written and/or verbal information is clear with a high caliber of mathematical reasoning
Product	Inappropriate product; does not show knowledge gained	Selected product is appropriate; needs further development to show knowledge gained	Acceptable and appropriate product; shows clear evidence of knowledge gained	Product is complex and shows evidence of internalization of mathematical & architectural concepts

Grade: _____

Comments: _____

_____

Figure 8.4. **Architecture rubric**

Note. Adapted from *Engaging Creative Thinking: Activities to Integrate Problem Solving,* by B. Kingore, 1998, Abilene, TX: Professional Associates Publishing. Copyright ©1998 by Professional Associates Publishing.

ogy by the end of the process even if their skills were only emerging at the beginning. This finding supports the idea that technology skills develop when they are used in authentic settings. Since this was a culminating activity for the architecture unit, I placed particular emphasis on the evaluation of the students' understanding of mathematical concepts and their completed product. The majority of the students also scored well in this area. Since they began the unit with little or no knowledge of architectural terms and concepts, I feel this level of student proficiency supported the NCTM belief that students learn best when they connect mathematical concepts to the real world (see Figure 8.5).

Conclusion

Incorporating technology into the mathematics curriculum in authentic ways encourages teachers of gifted learners to change their curriculum to meet the standards of reform initiatives. As students have experiences with technology that aid them in understanding topics in the core content areas and in applying those understandings to new situations, they will develop computer and problem-solving skills that will be needed in their future careers. Preparing gifted individuals to meet the challenges of the future should be a central goal of all gifted programs.

References

Christopher, M. (1998). Architecture. In B. Kingore, *Engaging creative thinking: Activities to integrate creative problem solving.* Abilene, TX: Professional Associates Publishing.

Commission on Standards for School Mathematics (CSSM). (1989). *Curriculum and evaluation standards for school mathematics.* Reston, VA: National Council of Teachers of Mathematics.

Division of Advanced Academic Services. (1996). *Texas state plan for the education of gifted/talented students.* Austin, TX: Texas Education Agency.

Kingore, B. (1998). *Engaging creative thinking: Activities to integrate creative problem solving.* Abilene, TX: Professional Associates

Grades 1–4	Grades 5–8
Mathematics as Problem Solving	*Mathematics as Problem Solving*
• use problem solving approaches to investigate and understand mathematical content	• use problem-solving approaches to investigate and understand mathematical content
• formulate problems from everyday and mathematical situations	• formulate problems from situations within and outside mathematics
Mathematical Connections	*Mathematical Connections*
• use mathematics in other curriculum areas	• apply mathematical thinking and modeling to solve problems that arise in others disciplines, such as art, music, psychology, science, and business
Geometry and Spatial Sense	
• describe, model, draw, and classify shapes	*Patterns and Functions*
• develop spatial sense	• describe, extend, analyze, and create a wide variety of patterns
• recognize and appreciate geometry in their world	• use patterns and functions to represent and solve problems
Patterns and Relationships	*Geometry*
• recognize, describe, extend, and create a wide variety of patterns	• identify, describe, compare, and classify geometric figures
	• visualize and represent geometric figures with special attention to developing spatial sense
	• represent and solve problems using geometric models
	• develop an appreciation of geometry as a means of describing the physical world

Figure 8.5. **NCTM Standards that support this performance task**

Publishing.

Panel on Education Technology of the President's Committee of Advisors on Science and Technology. (1997). *Report to the president on the use of technology to strengthen K–12 education in the United States*. Washington, DC: Executive Office of the President.

Resources

Abhau, M. (Ed.). (1986). *Architecture in education: A resource of imaginative ideas and tested activities*. Philadelphia, PA: Foundation for Architecture.

Blumenson, J. G. (1971). *Identifying American architecture: A pictorial guide to styles and terms, 1600–1945*. Nashville, TN: American Association for State and Local History.

Winters, N. B. (1986). *Architecture is elementary: Visual thinking through architectural concepts*. Salt Lake City, UT: Peregrine Smith Books.

chapter 9

Gifted Students Speak

mathematics problem-solving insights

by **Thomas R. Tretter**

One summer several years ago, I taught at the Governor's School of North Carolina, a 6-week residential program for academically or intellectually gifted rising high school seniors in North Carolina. Student eligibility for this program included multiple criteria: aptitude test scores in the 92nd–99th percentile; achievement test scores in the 92nd–99th percentile; scholastic performance records such as transcripts and class rank; and personal data such as school and community awards, honors, and activities (for more information, see http://www.ncgovschool.org). The intent of the academic program at the Governor's School was to challenge and stimulate these gifted students by emphasizing theory over memorization of fact, particularly contemporary and progressive theories that stimulate innovative thought in a rapidly changing culture.

To meet this goal for the Governor's School program, the curriculum had to be appropriate. Gallagher and Gallagher (1994) suggested four ways that a curriculum could be modified for gifted students: acceleration, enrichment, sophistication, and novelty. Coleman (2001) asserted that sophistication is what gifted students thrive on; but, of the four aforementioned modifications, it is the one that most often eludes teachers who attempt to modify curricula for gifted students. Because the unique environment of the Governor's School allowed the classroom teacher unusual flexibility in devising the curriculum, I concentrated on sophistication as I developed the curriculum for a 3-week session on mathematics problem solving.

A number of approaches to teaching mathematical problem solving are possible (e.g., Posamentier & Wolfgang, 1996). Kroll and Miller (1993) found that student beliefs about the processes of problem solving, ways to approach problem solving, and beliefs about their own ability to engage in problem solving may be important factors between successful and unsuccessful problem solvers. I developed a curriculum that integrated the five process standards espoused by the National Council of Teachers of Mathematics (NCTM, 2000): problem solving, reasoning and proof, communication, connections, and representations. My goal was to create a 3-week mathematics experience focusing on sophisticated mathematics that would engage gifted students in all of the process standards highlighted by the NCTM. My hope was that this experience would have a lasting impact on student beliefs about mathematics problem solving.

Course Content

The structure for the problem-solving course was to meet for 1 hour and 15 minutes once a day for 15 days spread over 3 weeks. One class of 15 students met in the morning, and a second class of 16 students met in the afternoon. In keeping with the overall goals of Governor's School, I wanted students to be able to take advantage of the numerous out-of-class activities, so I did not assign heavy workloads to be done outside the classroom. I designed a mathematics problem-solving curriculum emphasizing the following concepts:

- Understanding underlying mathematics is much more powerful for developing problem-solving capabilities than merely applying algorithms.

- Similar mathematical tools apply across a broad range of problems, even problems that may seem unrelated to each other.
- Mathematical analysis leads to useful insight in a wide variety of situations.

Many of the specific problems and situations I used to accomplish these goals are well-known to experienced mathematics teachers, but the manner of using them to highlight connections and complexity may not have been considered extensively. Along with a few administrative tasks related to students' mathematics journals and distribution of the first set of eight problems, the first day began with mathematics-oriented pictorial puzzles designed to stimulate creative thinking and to emphasize the value of teamwork. For example, a picture of a wavy line (a sine function) bisected horizontally by a dashed line represented "sine on the dotted line," and a picture of Santa Claus with "2L-2L" above his head represented "No L (Noel)."

As students pondered these pictorial puzzles, I encouraged them to say aloud any ideas they may have. Typically, a student would say something that wasn't completely correct, but that would stimulate another student to follow up on the idea that eventually led to a correct solution. I used this activity to emphasize the importance and usefulness of teamwork; without group contributions, it would usually be much more difficult and time-consuming to solve these puzzles. I strongly encouraged discussion and collaboration throughout the course, and this activity set the appropriate tone. Many of the students seemed to view teamwork and collaboration as an impediment to accomplishing mathematics tasks quickly, but perhaps they hadn't yet experienced enough of the kind of challenging mathematics tasks where the value of teamwork becomes evident.

The rest of the first day was devoted to students in teams of two solving a problem that didn't have any readily apparent mathematical equation or formula leading directly to a solution. (Figure 9.1 summarizes this problem.) As students worked on this task, they began to appreciate the value of developing their own notation systems and approaching the problem in an iterative sense. I challenged students who came up with a solution if they could do better. If not, I asked, how could they justify their solution as optimal?

Cori the camel lives at the edge of a large desert that is 1,000 miles across. Cori decides to take her banana harvest of 3,000 bananas to the faraway market that is 1,000 miles away on the other side of the desert. Cori can only carry a maximum of 1,000 bananas on her back at any one time, and she must eat one banana for every mile she travels. What is the greatest number of bananas that Cori can get to market?

Figure 9.1. **Cori the camel**

The next day, students continued with this problem, presenting solutions and ideas to the class. Typically, there were a number of different approaches and notation systems, and students began to appreciate different ways of thinking about the same situation. I then challenged the class to justify why a given solution was the optimal one. Usually, one or more groups had already made strides in this direction. With help, students were usually able to convince each other of an optimal solution of 533 bananas to market. Along the way, some algebraic equations were often generated, and students could see that sometimes a problem doesn't require the solver to search for an appropriate formula, but rather to create one of his or her own. I then asked students to generalize the solution to "beginning with x bananas, with the market y miles away, and Cori eating z bananas per mile traveled." Typically, I recommended they generalize one parameter at a time, work out a solution to that, and then add in another parameter. I used this to highlight the point that problem solving takes time, and sometimes it is helpful to begin with the specific and move toward the general case. The value of teamwork was again emphasized by this problem, with students benefiting from ideas presented by others.

The Cori the Camel activity demonstrated the value of understanding why a certain algorithm works to lead toward a solution, which led to the next part of the course. The next portion of the course, approximately 4–5 days long, was spent having students analyze why some very basic algorithms work. I had students explain the reasons behind subtraction techniques, including the little nines and ones put on top when borrowing.

They also described the reasons behind the algorithms for adding and multiplying fractions, as well as the algorithm for multiplication and division of multidigit numbers. In some cases, no student was able to explain an algorithm fully, providing me with an opportunity to do so. All these students could certainly do these problems effortlessly, but a number of them admitted to never having thought about why a given algorithm works.

I then taught students an algorithm to extract by hand the square root of a number to any desired degree of precision and asked them to explain why that procedure works. (See Figure 9.2 for this algorithm, and see http://MathCentral.uregina.ca/RR/database/RR.09.95/grzesina1.html for a geometric view why this algorithm works, or see http://jwilson.coe.uga.edu/EMT668/EMAT6680.F99/Challen/squareroot/sqrt.html for an algebraic perspective.) This square root algorithm was chosen in order to have students think about something that most have never seen before, in contrast to explaining procedures they already knew very well. With a little practice, students could easily apply the algorithm, but they had a difficult time explaining why it worked. With extensive guidance from me, students eventually grasped the mathematical foundations behind the algorithm. Many of them told me that, although they had been good at doing these sorts of computations since elementary school, they had never thought about why they work and were surprised at the depth of understanding needed in order to understand the algorithms fully.

To show that algorithms can be taught and learned at mathematical levels higher than elementary arithmetic, I then taught students a beginning calculus example: how to take the derivative of a polynomial function, a topic presented in any first-year calculus text. Although some had already seen this in their previous math courses, others had not. This algorithm is much simpler than the square root algorithm, and, within a few minutes, all the students could easily apply it. However, they couldn't explain why the procedure produced the derivative of the function.

In order for them to understand this procedure fully, I first had to detour into teaching (or reviewing, depending on the student's background) about permutations, combinations, and

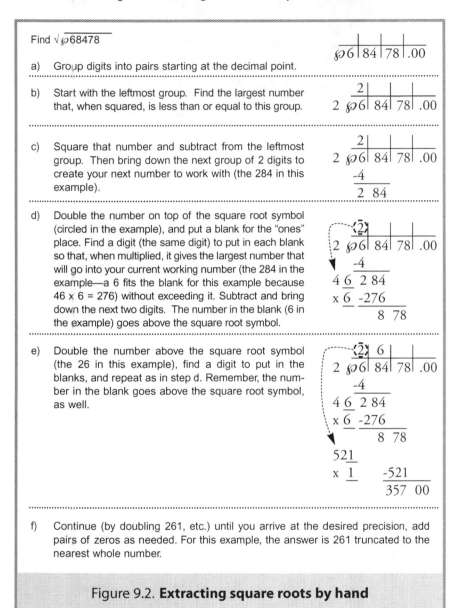

Find $\sqrt{68478}$

a)   Group digits into pairs starting at the decimal point.

b)   Start with the leftmost group. Find the largest number that, when squared, is less than or equal to this group.

c)   Square that number and subtract from the leftmost group. Then bring down the next group of 2 digits to create your next number to work with (the 284 in this example).

d)   Double the number on top of the square root symbol (circled in the example), and put a blank for the "ones" place. Find a digit (the same digit) to put in each blank so that, when multiplied, it gives the largest number that will go into your current working number (the 284 in the example—a 6 fits the blank for this example because 46 x 6 = 276) without exceeding it. Subtract and bring down the next two digits. The number in the blank (6 in the example) goes above the square root symbol.

e)   Double the number above the square root symbol (the 26 in this example), find a digit to put in the blanks, and repeat as in step d. Remember, the number in the blank goes above the square root symbol, as well.

f)   Continue (by doubling 261, etc.) until you arrive at the desired precision, add pairs of zeros as needed. For this example, the answer is 261 truncated to the nearest whole number.

Figure 9.2. **Extracting square roots by hand**

the binomial theorem. I highlighted the strong connection between combinations and the binomial theorem, pointing out how the coefficients from the binomial theorem can be thought of as coming from computations of combinations (see Figure 9.3 for an example).

The binomial theorem expands binomials of the form $(x + h)^n$.

Example: $(x + h)^3 = (x + h)(x + h)(x + h) = 1x^3 + 3x^2h + 3xh^2 + 1h^3$.

In order to carry out this multiplication by hand, essentially each term in a factor must be multiplied with each other term in the other factors and then collected like terms. The first coefficient of 1 can be thought of as the number of ways of choosing zero of the h's out of the three available (only one way to do this: choose only the x's) because the h factor is to the zeroth power in that term of the expansion, or in the notation of combinatorics, the number of ways to choose 0 from 3 choices is $\binom{3}{0} = 1$. The second coefficient of 3 can be thought of as the number of ways of choosing one of the h's out of the three available, $\binom{3}{1} = 3$. There are three ways because you can choose the one h (only one h because it is to the first power in this term) to be from each factor in turn. Similarly, the third coefficient has h^2, and so the number of ways to choose two h's out of three available is $\binom{3}{2} = 3$, and the last term of the expansion chooses all three of the three h's available, $\binom{3}{3} = 1$. In general, for the nth power, the coefficients of the expansion are given by $\binom{n}{0}\binom{n}{1}\binom{n}{2} \cdots \binom{n}{n-2}\binom{n}{2}$ These coefficients can be arranged in a triangular form, each row representing the next higher power of the exponent n, starting with $n = 0$. This arrangement of coefficients is called Pascal's Triangle.

$(x + h)^0$						1				
$(x + h)^1$					1		1			
$(x + h)^2$				1		2		1		
$(x + h)^3$			1		3		3		1	
$(x + h)^4$		1		4		6		4		1
$(x + h)^5$	1		5		10		10		5		1

Figure 9.3. **Combinations and the binomial theorem**

I then used a definition of a derivative to be a limit of the slope of a function and demonstrated to the students how the list of simple rules given earlier, when applied to a polynomial, will produce the derivative. This definition included a binomial term, and the mathematics simplified to the point where the second number in the given row of Pascal's Triangle turned out to play an important role (see Figure 9.3). The link between Pascal's Triangle, combinatorics, and derivatives was used to develop the simple rules that took only a few minutes to master 2 days earlier. I pointed out to the students that I could teach them *how* to take a derivative in minutes, but that to truly *understand* it took 2 days of preliminary background.

While we were examining these various algorithms over the course of a week, students were working on the first problem set given out on the first day. As they brought questions to class, we would address them, which allowed students to have input into the topics considered day to day. The problems on this problem set were designed to utilize the mathematics discussed during the algorithm problems, as well as expose students to potentially new areas of mathematics such as modular arithmetic (see Figure 9.4 for a few sample problems from this set).

Sample problem 1 in Figure 9.4 stimulated thinking related to modular arithmetic, and, once students had a chance to discuss this problem in class and see approaches taken by others, they were usually able to solve it. Part (b) of this problem asked them to generalize their solution strategy, which required them to understand more deeply what was driving their solution. As always, I stressed the mathematical thinking, not the specific answer. The second sample problem afforded multiple solution paths, which provided for interesting classroom discussion. Students might simply look for a pattern, which is all that is actually asked for. They could then write their solution as a sum of terms. They could also recognize that the triangular numbers, which incidentally show up in Pascal's Triangle in the second diagonal (1, 3, 6, 10, . . .), are in the pattern (see Figure 9.3). Use of the triangular numbers combined with formulas developed earlier for combinations led to a closed form solution for sample problem 2 in set 1. Students usually ended up at different points on these solution spectra, and classroom discussions of the thinking that went into various approaches often proved insightful for all students. The value of previous knowledge applied to a problem that seemed completely different from the initial context of exposure to Pascal's Triangle intrigued many students. After

1. a) Two cyclists are racing on a circular track, but are moving in opposite directions. Their speeds are 15 m/s and 21 m/s. They start at the same time and place, and they finish when they simultaneously meet at the starting point again. Excluding the start and finish, how many times will they pass each other during the course of the race?

   b) Develop a solution strategy for the general case where person 1 travels at x m/s and person 2 at y m/s.

2. Start with one hexagon ($n = 1$) and surround it with six hexagons ($n = 2$). Then, surround it with more hexagons ($n = 3$), etc. Find an expression for the total number of hexagons in this pattern in terms of n.

Figure 9.4. **Sample items from problem set 1**

about two class periods were spent on this problem set, students began to appreciate the value of experience in a variety of mathematical thought because very diverse problems could often be attacked with similar thinking. Although it took some time to follow the mathematical detour for understanding the algorithm for taking derivatives of polynomials, the knowledge gained by this detour turned out to be useful in other contexts.

The second half of the course was spent showing how mathematics could be used to analyze a variety of situations. Students were given a second problem set of nine problems in order to establish a common base for future class discussions (Figure 9.5 shows a few sample problems from this set). Many of these problems were again carefully chosen to use prior topics we had discussed, as well as stretch students' mathematical experiences in new directions. Part (b) of the first problem leads to a result called Gomory's Theorem, but is something that offers multiple opportunities to seek a solution. The last three sample problems all can be solved with techniques that relate back to Pascal's Triangle. The seeming disparity in those problems hides some underlying commonalities. As with the first problem set, students worked on these problems throughout the second half of the course, bringing questions and ideas to class to bounce off of each other as needed.

The second portion of the course analyzed the well-known Tower of Hanoi problem (see Figure 9.6). Students were given

1. a) Suppose we are given an ordinary 8 x 8 chessboard and 32 dominoes of dimensions 2 x 1. Obviously, the dominoes can be arranged on the board to cover it completely. Now, two opposite corner squares of the chessboard are cut away, and one domino is discarded. The problem is to determine whether or not the remaining 31 dominoes can be arranged on the reduced board so as to cover it exactly.

    b) Determine an algorithm to remove two squares that will <u>always</u> allow you to cover the remaining board with the 31 dominoes.

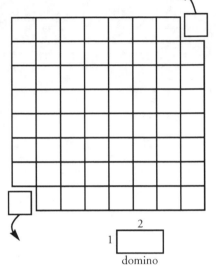

2. In the diagram, the product of the six entries in Pascal's Triangle surrounding the first 4 is a perfect square; this is,1 x 3 x 6 x 10 x 5 x 1 = 900 = 30². Show that the product of the six entries surrounding any interior entry in Pascal's Triangle is a perfect square.

3. How many even five-digit numbers have the property that the sum of the first four digits is the units digit?

4. What is the millionth term in the sequence 1, 2, 2, 3, 3, 3, 4, 4, 4, 4, . . . ?

Figure 9.5. **Sample items from problem set 2**

manipulatives to use if needed, and they suggested starting with a small number and building up a pattern. Students worked with recursive formulas to solve this problem and then translated that recursive formula into a closed form solution. With classmates, students were generally able to do this, and so I then

In an ancient city in India, so the legend goes, monks in a temple have to move a pile of 64 sacred disks from one location to another. The disks are fragile; only one can be carried at a time. A disk may not be placed on top of a smaller, less valuable disk. And there is only one other location in the temple (besides the original and destination locations) sacred enough that a pile of disks can be placed there. So, the monks start moving disks back and forth between the original pile, the destination pile, and the intermediate location, always keeping piles in order of largest on the bottom and smallest on top. How many moves will the monks have to make to complete the transfer of these 64 disks?

Figure 9.6. **Tower of Hanoi problem**

challenged them to develop closed form solutions for more general linear recursive formulas. This led to much more complexity and special conditions that needed to be applied in some cases. This activity not only introduced students to thinking recursively, but also to appreciate again the value of teamwork, the value of starting simple and building up to more complex situations, and the ubiquity of some basic mathematical processes useful for approaching a variety of problem situations.

During this portion of the course, students also explored computational science techniques as an approach to problem solving. The Web site http://www.shodor.org/interactivate/activities/index.html provides a number of applications appropriate for experimentation with ideas related to fractals, chaos theory, and probability, among others. These activities exposed students to the idea that not all of mathematics leads to closed form solutions or explicit equations, but mathematical ideas can still be useful for solving a wide variety of problems.

In the second half of the course, students also analyzed a game strategy for a number of different games such as Sprouts (see Figure 9.7). Both recursive thinking and portions of Pascal's triangle are relevant in the analysis of strategy for winning this game, helping students to see that mathematical knowledge applied in one context can reappear in seemingly unrelated areas. As time permitted, various games were mathematically analyzed for strategy. Rudimentary graph theory problems were also introduced. The final few days were again spent discussing

For two players. Rules:
1. Begin with a given number of dots, keeping the number relatively small to limit the duration of the game.
2. On your turn, connect dots with an arc. An arc can connect any two dots subject to the restrictions below.
3. An arc can connect a dot to itself.
4. A new dot is placed at the midpoint of each new arc.
5. No dot can have more than three arcs coming from it.
6. No arc can cross another arc.
7. The winner is the player who makes the last valid move.

Sample game with three starting dots (new moves each turn are shown dashed.)

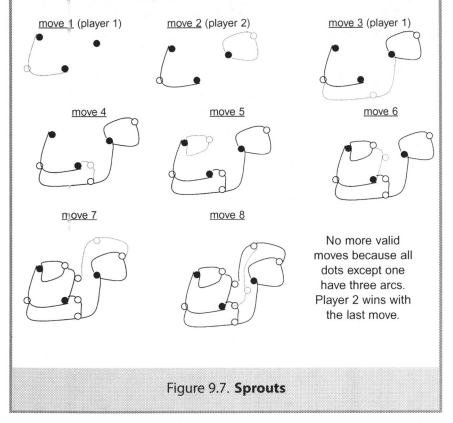

move 1 (player 1)   move 2 (player 2)   move 3 (player 1)

move 4   move 5   move 6

move 7   move 8

No more valid moves because all dots except one have three arcs. Player 2 wins with the last move.

Figure 9.7. **Sprouts**

any of the questions from problem set 2 that had not yet been resolved.

In general, throughout the course, not only were students exposed to mathematical thinking in a variety of situations, but they also got to see how some of the same mathematical ideas used earlier were useful in new situations. I chose to use Pascal's Triangle as one of my unifying themes because of its versatility, but other choices are also possible. As the reader may notice, the number of different problems attempted was relatively small for such a mathematically capable group of students. However, I attempted to include a representative sample of problems from different mathematical branches so that students could gain some appreciation of the breadth of mathematical thinking, as well as the depth. The goal was to balance breadth and depth of mathematical topics within a short 3-week session without sacrificing too much of either one.

Student Voices

As current reform efforts strive to make curricula more student-centered (NCTM, 2000; National Research Council, 1996), one group that may nevertheless be overlooked is student input into the curriculum and its implementation. Student voices are sometimes absent from discussions of school policies and practices. Nieto (1994) highlighted this deficiency and argued for the importance of students having input into schooling processes, particularly students from backgrounds typically considered out of the mainstream. Gifted students, while not specifically mentioned by Nieto, may also fall into a category out of the mainstream, not having their voices heard on curricular matters of importance to them. Hatchman and Rolland (2001) recommended that educators and policy makers listen to student voices in order to implement school reform effectively. They argued that such input is extremely helpful in creating schools where students thrive academically. Kordalewski (1999) summarizes specific teaching strategies that may help encourage this input from students, reflecting a growing movement to consider what students have to say as being important.

There is a continuing need to highlight the importance of student voices in research. "Virtually no research has been done that places student experience at the center of attention. . . . Rarely is the perspective of the student herself explored" (Erickson & Schultz, 1992, p. 467). This article attempts to address this void, providing a forum for gifted students' voices to be heard concerning their reactions to the mathematics problem-solving course they experienced at the Governor's School. Students themselves may be the best judges of the effectiveness of a curriculum and its implementation, and they may provide guidance on aspects helpful to consider for future courses.

In order to evaluate the success of this endeavor to create a course with more mathematical sophistication than often seen in regular high school courses, I asked students to respond in writing to several questions (see Figure 9.8). These prompts were provided to aid in developing introductions to the mathematics journals the students had been keeping throughout the course. Students were encouraged to limit this introduction to one page in an attempt to distill their main thoughts down to the most important ideas.

A content analysis of the students' responses to these prompts and their own unsolicited comments about the course revealed some interesting themes that provide insight into what these gifted students value in an educational setting for the learning of mathematics. A total of 28 students responded to these prompts, but not all students responded to all of them. Here is what they said.

Student Comments

Prompt 1: What abilities are important for someone to become an adept mathematics problem solver in situations that may arise in genuine contexts?

In response to prompt 1, the most common theme that emerged (12 students) was to emphasize the importance of understanding *why*, instead of merely *how*. A. H. expressed this emphasis by writing, "Understanding math is much more important than being able to complete 60 math problems correctly. I have learned that the thought process is very important and that now more than ever I must become responsible for my learning." Some students were surprised to learn that they really didn't understand very rudimentary mathematics on a deep level. For example, M. L. wrote, "Basic, fundamental principles are examined in new lights to my amazement when I realized

1. What abilities are important for someone to become an adept mathematics problem solver in situations that may arise in genuine contexts?

2. Has this course helped you think about mathematics differently than a typical high school course might have, and what are your opinions about any differences?

3. Would you recommend a similar course to other high school seniors?

4. What would be the most important idea(s) that a reader should get from reading your journal?

Figure 9.8. **Prompts provided to solicit student responses in their mathematics journals**

that I can do and understand differential equations, but not arithmetic. Thank you for expanding my mind." The course emphasis on the importance of the process that leads to understanding, as opposed to the product that results from mindlessly applying an algorithm, is reflected in L. E.'s comment, "The thinking is more important than the product."

A second common theme emerging from this prompt (7 students) was the need to be able to think creatively, to not be artificially restricted in strategies for solving problems. R. Y.'s comment, "[This course gave me] strength to realize that it's OK to be wrong; being wrong on one thing can bring you a right answer on another thing," highlighted the value of making mistakes and going down dead-end pathways on the way to improving mathematical problem-solving skills. The creative aspect of mathematics came to the fore in K. W.'s assertion, "To be a good problem solver, one must think 'outside the box'— think deeper than usual."

Prompt 2: Has this course helped you think about mathematics differently than a typical high school course might have, and what are your opinions about any differences?

In response to prompt 2, student comments clustered into three themes: most high school courses and textbooks don't go deep enough (8 students), problem solving takes time that is not usually made available in most high school courses (5 students), and most high school courses are concerned with preparing you for the test, not for understanding (4 students).

Criticism of the lack of depth in high school courses centered on both the activities implemented by the teacher and the textbooks and other resources used. "In high school, [the teachers] rarely say why [mathematical algorithms] work. Now I know to either question why, or to figure it out myself." This response from C. M. indicated a realization that he could take some of his learning into his own hands if he were unsatisfied with what a course offered—a powerful recognition of the ability to control one's own learning. Not only are classroom activities criticized for not going deep enough, but textbooks received similar criticism. According to L. S., "Textbook questions are sometimes rather basic and don't require deep thinking."

The second theme emerging from this prompt concerned the lack of time in most courses. R. F. recognized the value and need for adequate time, writing, "Problem solving takes time. It isn't always simple questions you can answer off the top of your head." M. J. contrasted her Governor's School experience of mathematical problem solving with her experiences in her high school, also focusing on the valuable resource of time: "This is definitely not a high school course, for the simple reason that [in high school] there's not enough time or not enough teachers willing to go through with [the extensive development of a mathematical idea]."

The third theme arising from this prompt revealed some interesting insights about how testing can detract from a course's value. T. M.'s view that "high school courses are too vague. They don't go deep, just try to quickly prepare you for the test" attributed the lack of depth of high school mathematics courses at least partly to testing pressure. A. H. expressed a similar view: "In a typical high school math class, there is such a narrow focus that you are learning math simply for the test, not for later applications." J. L. equated the absence of testing at the Governor's School with educational value: "My high school teachers do not explore why. Most importantly, I will remember the testless, fully educational, non-pressure-giving courses this summer." Student comments falling under this theme expressed a common sentiment that much of testing is detrimental to the educational value of their coursework in their home high schools.

Prompt 3: Would you recommend a similar course to other high school seniors?

In response to prompt 3, students strongly recommended (16 students) a similar course for all students, regardless of their mathematical ability. C. R. believed such an approach would even help students who may not have a mathematical inclination: "I would recommend this class to anyone willing to learn more math to help them with any type of problem, not just math-oriented people, but anybody." These gifted students seemed to find the approach taken in this course to be beneficial to them, and many believed that other students would likewise benefit from such an approach. B. L. highlighted the emphasis on thinking as particularly beneficial: "I think [this course] was very beneficial to me and everyone should be exposed to this kind of thinking." Similar sentiments expressed by many students underlined the potential for an appropriate emphasis in mathematics courses to impact positively the learning of a wide spectrum of students.

Prompt 4: What would be the most important idea(s) that a reader should get from reading your journal?

Many of the most important ideas listed in the responses to prompt 4 included themes already discussed. In addition, a number of students mentioned that they really enjoyed the challenge (7 students) and that they better understood the rich tapestry of mathematics as it relates to applications in the real world (7 students). Many students discussed the exposure to really thinking about underlying mathematics and connections between seemingly different applications as part of the most important and enjoyable aspect of this course. T. H. expressed this by writing, "Problem-solving class helped me to think this year. It was one of the best things at Governor's School." L. E. focused on the challenging aspect of the course: "This course offered me a great challenge and has done as much for me in 3 weeks as a typical high school course would." M. A. expressed her enjoyment: "It is really fun thinking through things."

Comments pertaining to the connections between mathematics and applications, as well as connections within the field of mathematics itself, were also seen as important aspects of the course. K. T. revealed a surprising gap in her mathematical experience considering that she had had formal schooling in mathematics for at least 11 years: "I've never had to think about math as it relates to everyday life." The use of mathematics to analyze applications different from most test questions may have prompted C. K. to write, "Problem-solving is much more difficult in real life than it is on tests." The opportunity for student input into the direction of classroom discussions and input into time spent on portions of mathematics that interested them was appreciated by students such as K. T., who wrote, "I was glad that [the teacher] would get into math tangents that interested him and us." This approach allowed the rich interconnections between mathematical topics to be explored as class interest dictated, which helped to illuminate the existence of connections of which students may not have previously been aware.

The students in this program were successful problem solvers in order to be eligible for the Governor's School program. In spite of this success, many of them expressed a common faulty impression that all mathematics problems could be solved quickly and directly. For example, A. F. wrote in his mathematics journal, "Not all problems can be solved, and the person who tries the most and takes the most time is usually the one who gets the answer. I used to think that, if I took longer than about 15 minutes on a problem, I must have been doing it wrong and I felt stupid. Now I realize that there are some problems that require time to solve."

Students also tended to believe that there was one right way to solve a given problem, a common misconception highlighted by Kroll and Miller (1993). After the experience of this problem-solving course, H. R. described a shift away from this misconception: "The questions in real life are so much more complex than those encountered in most courses." These types of student comments suggest that, in spite of these students being among the most mathematically able high school seniors in North Carolina, they had not truly experienced much sophisticated mathematics that would challenge their misconceptions. If, as Halmos (1980) suggested, problem solving is the heart of mathematics, then even these mathematically gifted students, on the cusp of their last year in high school, may not have yet developed this core skill to their full potential.

Discussion of Student Comments

Coleman's (2001) assertion that bringing more complexity and abstraction to a subject (sophistication) is needed to meet the desires of gifted students seems to be supported by these student comments. Some models of curricular modification for gifted students focus on content acceleration and fast-paced instruction. For example, McCarthy (1998) researched a model whereby middle school students complete 4 years of high school math in 2 years during their regular school day. While such models certainly have a valuable role to play in educating gifted students, student comments in the previous section reinforce the idea that modification via sophistication, rather than acceleration, may be an effective way to motivate gifted students. None of the students complained, either in journal writing or informally in conversation, about the pace of the class or the amount of content coverage. In fact, many of them indicated that they particularly enjoyed exploring fewer topics in more depth.

As I read the students' journals, I was struck by the overwhelming sense of excitement and energy as they wrote about the abstraction and depth provided throughout the course; this aspect is what seemed to capture their interest. A theme that emerged was the desire to have more time to study topics in depth, which supports Kaplan's (2001) call for educators to become advocates for creating the time gifted students need for optimal learning. Student comments about time and the focus of classroom instruction due to tests also have implications for the trend of ever-increasing standardized testing in our educational system. These comments highlight the danger that ill-considered testing may rob our most capable students of an appropriate curricular approach. Strong advocates in this arena are needed to ensure that gifted students (as well as other students) do not lose out on appropriate instruction.

Another aspect of this experience that may have contributed to the students' positive responses was the collaborative nature of the course. The scoring procedures of standardized tests such as the SAT compare students to one another, which implies an inherently competitive framework. All the students at the Governor's School score well on standardized tests in order to be eligible for the program, which may indicate a propensity to consider schooling as an academically competitive activity. In contrast to competition, I encouraged cooperation and collaboration throughout the course.

Diezmann and Watters (2001) found that gifted students preferred collaboration to independent work only when the task was sufficiently challenging. As in their study, student collaboration in this course was self-initiated, as opposed to teacher-directed. Although formal cooperative learning groups were not assigned, students were encouraged to work together by discussing approaches and thoughts related to the mathematics being studied. Garduno (2001) likewise found that gifted students were more motivated when they were able to advance at their own pace, were grouped with others of similar ability, and were engaged with tasks involving complex processes, as opposed to merely computational procedures. The structure of the Governor's School program, wherein gifted students are all housed together in a dormitory setting 7 days a week throughout the course, seemed to be conducive to collaboration, as evidenced by student comments about working together on problems. A number of student comments pointed out the insight gained by seeing other students' thought processes and expressed appreciation for the opportunity to do so. Students were able to establish the pace of their work to some extent because they had significant input into the daily topics and particular problems addressed in class. The admissions requirements for the Governor's School ensured that all students in the class were of similar mathematical ability, and the course intentionally focused on complex mathematical processes, as opposed to merely computational procedures. This confluence of conditions satisfied those highlighted by Garduno, and students' comments imply a high degree of motivation on their part.

Conclusions

All of the students quoted in this article had already completed precalculus in their home high school before enrolling in the Governor's School, and some had completed as much as 2 years of calculus along with additional advanced math courses offered through local universities. Although such advanced high school math courses are intended to serve academically gifted students, student comments indicated that educators may need to consider modifications to such courses to stimulate our academically gifted students. It may be valuable to offer 3-week intensive courses somewhat similar to the one offered by this author—it should be possible to carve this time out of traditional advanced mathematics courses and still have gifted students do well on standardized tests. If this practice were to become a norm, gifted students may discover the challenge and beauty of mathematics that many indicated was lacking through their regular high school courses.

To have an even greater impact than a separate short course, incorporating the pedagogical characteristics appreciated and highlighted by these gifted students into regular coursework is not only possible, but also recommended by national mathematics standards. These students indicated that a similar experience would be appropriate and helpful for all kinds of students, not just the most academically capable. This philosophy of providing enriching mathematics for all students, termed the equity principle, is a centerpiece of the national mathematics principles and standards (NCTM, 2000, pp. 12–14).

The comments from the students can be synthesized into three broad recommendations for modifications and changes in emphasis to existing traditional mathematics courses:

1. more emphasis on *why*, instead of *how*, something is done;
2. more depth, less breadth of coverage; and
3. more challenge.

One aspect of this experience that was greatly appreciated and recommended by these students was the focus on having them understand *why* certain mathematical approaches or algorithms are used as opposed to merely *how*. This recommendation is directly aligned with the learning principle espoused by the national mathematics standards (NCTM, 2000, pp. 20–21) that states that students must learn mathematics with understanding. This emphasis should be incorporated into any mathematics course. Although it undoubtedly takes more time to delve into the *why*, the payoff comes in student interest and understanding of the underlying mathematics. Even if such an approach couldn't be done for every topic in a course's curriculum due to time constraints, perhaps it could be done occasionally. The impression given by these students is that this is a rare to nonexistent approach in their mathematics experiences.

A second student theme that deserves more attention in many mathematics courses is to focus more on depth and less on breadth of coverage. This point is also made in several well-respected documents, including national science standards that point out that "the present curricula in science and mathematics are overstuffed and undernourished" (AAAS, 1989, p. 14); a Third International Mathematics and Science Study (TIMSS) report from a comparison of mathematics and science programs worldwide that states, "[The United States'] curricula, textbooks, and teaching all are 'a mile wide and an inch deep'" (McNeely, 1997, p. 161); and national mathematics standards that advocate for a coherent, focused, and well-articulated curriculum (NCTM, 2000, pp. 14–16.) Many students seemed to appreciate the opportunity to investigate a few mathematical ideas in depth, in the process uncovering connections between seemingly disparate mathematical ideas. Again, this modification requires time, a precious commodity in a classroom, but one that should be spent in the most productive ways. Such a change in focus away from breadth toward depth seems likely to be a productive use of this finite resource. There is much to recommend in sophistication of content over broad coverage of it.

Thirdly, these students relished the challenge presented. Mathematical ideas that were presented in ways that were nontrivial both engaged and frustrated the students—a situation ripe for learning. Part of the national mathematics standards' teaching principle highlights the need to challenge students (NCTM, 2000, pp. 16–19.) The collaborative nature of classroom discussions of mathematical problems and presentations of students' disparate ideas on how to attack these various problems seemed to both alleviate the frustration and increase student engagement. In the process of wrestling with various challenging problems, students came to appreciate the rich tapestry of mathematical ideas. They appreciated the value of building new concepts on existing ones and looking for connections between problems. A pedagogical approach highlighting connections and encouraging wrestling with challenging problems over an extended period of time should be incorporated at the appropriate level into any mathematics class. Once students realize that they will not be penalized for not immediately knowing how to solve a given problem, they may enjoy the prospect of tackling challenging problems in collaboration with their peers.

These three recommendations from the students, which are also emphasized by current reform documents, are actually mutually supporting. If a curriculum were to focus more on depth and less on breadth of coverage, this would provide time to emphasize the *why* of something more than merely *how*. This emphasis, in turn, would lead to more challenging content for the students. These recommendations are therefore not unattainable; they do, however, require some serious restructuring of the mathematics curriculum.

Some research indicates that having participated in a gifted program in high school does not result in increased university achievement. Grayson (2001) studied the achievement of students over the course of 4 years at a university in Ontario and compared achievement of those students who graduated from high school having participated in gifted programs with those who had not. He found no differences in university achievement between the two groups and attributed this lack of difference to the possibility that the selection process for identifying gifted students may be flawed. An alternative explanation not discussed by Grayson is that perhaps the differentiated instruction received by students identified as gifted was ineffective. Student insights and comments reported in this article suggest that mathematics instruction they received in their high school courses may not be helping them reach their high academic potential. Perhaps educators need to rethink how and why we provide instruction for our gifted high school students in order to have the most powerful impact on their learning.

Educators of gifted students need to be strong advocates for practices that best serve these academically capable students. The best guidance on what is important often comes from the students themselves. The congruence between recommendations of the national mathematics standards and recommendations of these students for effective mathematics curricula serves to emphasize the need to enact these reforms. Students are telling us what they want and need in order to be challenged and stimulated; it is up to us to listen to them and act. M. L.'s closing remark in the introduction to her mathematics journal clearly states this desire: "I have always wanted to have someone instruct me on the ways of the mind."

Can we fulfill such a request?

References

American Association for the Advancement of Science (AAAS). (1989). *Science for all Americans.* Washington, DC: Author.

Coleman, M. R. (2001). Curriculum differentiation: Sophistication. *Gifted Child Today, 24*(2), 24–25.

Diezmann, C., & Watters, J. (2001). The collaboration of mathematically gifted students on challenging tasks. *Journal for the Education of the Gifted, 25,* 7–31.

Erickson, F., & Schultz, J. (1992). Students' experience of the curriculum. In P. W. Jackson (Ed.), *Handbook of research on curriculum* (pp. 465–485). New York: Macmillan.

Gallagher, J., & Gallagher, S. (1994). *Teaching the gifted child* (4th ed.). Boston: Allyn and Bacon.

Garduno, E. (2001). The influence of cooperative problem solving on gender differences in achievement, self-efficacy, and attitudes toward mathematics in gifted students. *Gifted Child Quarterly, 45,* 268–282.

Grayson, J. P. (2001). The performance of "gifted" high school students in university. *Canadian Journal of Higher Education, 31*(1), 121–139.

Halmos, P. R. (1980). The heart of mathematics. *American Mathematical Monthly, 87*(7), 519–524.

Hatchman, J., & Rolland, C. (2001). *Students' voices about schooling: What works for them—its implications to school reform.* (ERIC Document Reproduction Service No. ED457576)

Kaplan, S. N. (2001). It's time. *Gifted Child Today, 24*(2), 31.

Kordalewski, J. (1999). *Incorporating student voice into teaching practice.* Washington, DC: ERIC Clearinghouse on Teaching and Teacher Education (ERIC Document Reproduction Service No. ED440049)

Kroll, D., & Miller, T. (1993). Insights from research on mathematical problem solving in the middle grades. In D. T. Owens (Ed.), *Research ideas for the classroom: Middle grades mathematics* (pp. 58–77). New York: Macmillan.

McCarthy, C. (1998). Assimilating the talent search model into the school day. *Journal of Secondary Gifted Education, 9,* 114–123.

McNeely, M. (Ed.). (1997). *Guidebook to examine school curricula.* Washington, DC: U.S. Department of Education, Office of Educational Research and Improvement.

National Council of Teachers of Mathematics (NCTM). (2000). *Principles and standards for school mathematics.* Reston, VA: Author.

National Research Council. (1996). *National science education standards.* Washington, DC: National Academy Press.

Nieto, S. (1994). Lessons from students on creating a chance to dream. *Harvard Educational Review, 64,* 392–426.

Posamentier, A., & Wolfgang, S. (1996). *The art of problem solving: A resource for the mathematics teacher.* Thousand Oaks, CA: Corwin Press. (ERIC Document Reproduction Service No. ED391689)

About the Authors

Cheryll M. Adams is director of the Center for Gifted Studies and Talent Development at Ball State University.

Mary M. Christopher serves as assistant professor in educational studies at Hardin-Simmons University. Previously, she taught for more than 15 years in elementary and middle schools in Texas, Oklahoma, and Kentucky.

Marc Curliss is the lead math and science specialist at the Education Service Center–Region 12. His major duties include planning and presenting K–12 math and science professional development for a region that is made up of 78 school districts in Central Texas.

Carmel Diezmann is a mathematics education lecturer at Queensland University of Technology in Brisbane, Australia.

Susan E. Fello is an assistant professor at Indiana University of Pennsylvania. Previously, she taught in public schools for 30 years, providing enrichment support services for elementary gifted and talented students, focusing on mathematics and language arts.

Todd Kettler is the director of advanced academic studies for the Waco Independent School District in Waco, TX. He also teaches courses in gifted education in the School of Education at Baylor University.

Rebecca L. Pierce is an associate professor in the Department of Mathematical Sciences at Ball State University.

Jennifer V. Rotigel is an associate professor at Indiana University of Pennsylvania and chairperson of the Department of Professional Studies in Education. She is currently writing a book titled *The Involved Parents Guide to Encouraging Your Child's Math Ability*, which will be published by Prufrock Press in 2005.

Catherine Finlayson Reed teaches the Elementary Mathematics Methods course at California State University–Hayward for the Multiple Subjects Credential Program. She also teaches in the Master of Science in Curriculum and Instruction program, where she is involved with the students who have opted for the Mathematics Concentration and teaches Error Patterns in Mathematics and Advanced Curriculum in Mathematics.

Sylvia St. Cyr is a gifted education specialist. She teaches mathematics and technology to all fourth- through sixth-grade students and pull-out instruction to third- through sixth-grade gifted students at Hilltop Elementary School in Reading, OH.

Susan Lee Stutler is a teacher and the program coordinator for gifted education in Phoenix, AZ.

Thomas R. Tretter is an assistant professor of science education at the University of Louisville.

James J. Watters is coordinator of graduate studies in the Faculty of Education at Queensland University of Technology in Brisbane, Australia. He is also coeditor of the *Australasian Journal for Gifted Education* and has served in an advisory capacity on gifted education for the state Education Department.

Printed in the United States
by Baker & Taylor Publisher Services